The Catechism of Virtues

The Teachings of Blessed Francisco Palau y Quer

Translation by Saul Cross

The Catechism of Virtues

The Teachings of Blessed Francisco Palau y Quer

Copyright 2023. Motmot.org

Contents

Introduction

"The Catechism of Virtue" by Father Francisco Palau y Quer provides an insightful journey into the essence of virtues and their central role in the spiritual life. The author's story, which is steeped in both spiritual exploration and societal upheaval, uniquely informs the narrative and gives readers a fresh perspective on the timeless subject of virtue.

Born on December 29, 1811, in Aitona, Lerida, Francisco Palau y Quer was the seventh child of a humble farming family rooted in their Catholic faith. The socio-political turbulence of the Peninsular War in Spain was the backdrop of his early life. Despite the chaos, young Palau found solace in his spiritual calling and decided to become a priest at the age of 14. His seminary studies brought him into the fold of the Discalced Carmelite friars, a religious order he joined in 1832.

His pursuit of religious life coincided with the First Carlist War, which sparked widespread religious persecution in Spain. Despite the dangerous times, Palau remained steadfast in his commitment. He was ordained a priest in 1836 while in exile, away from his Carmelite community. His early years of priesthood were characterized by itinerant preaching and time spent in solitude, living in the caves of Catalonia and Aragon.

Palau's life took another turn in 1840 when the royalist forces in Berga were defeated. Anticipating retribution from the Liberal authorities, he went into exile in France. There, Palau's deep connection with solitude and asceticism continued to flourish. He lived in caves, wrote religious texts, and inspired groups of men and women to adopt similar ascetic lifestyles.

In 1851, following a Concordat between the Spanish government and the Holy See, Palau returned to Spain. Despite his inability to live in a religious community, he remained active in the Church, serving as a spiritual director to seminarians and organizing the School of Virtue in Barcelona.

His return to Spain was marked by additional trials, including banishment to the island of Ibiza, where he spent six years. However, even during this challenging period, his spiritual zeal remained undimmed. He established a hermitage, promoted devotion to the Blessed Virgin Mary, and founded the Congregation - Third Order of Discalced Carmelites of the Congregation of Spain.

The last years of Palau's life were characterized by an outpouring of spiritual creativity and service. He wrote a Rule of Life and Constitutions for the Discalced Carmelite Third Order, assisted the sick during a typhus outbreak, and practiced exorcism. His life came to a peaceful end on March 20, 1872, after falling ill with pneumonia.

In 1988, the Catholic Church beatified Francisco Palau y Quer, acknowledging his lifelong dedication to spirituality and service. The legacy of his teachings and practices continue to inspire and guide countless individuals on their spiritual journeys.

This book, "The Catechism of Virtue", encapsulates the profound spiritual insights of Father Francisco Palau, shaped by his extraordinary life experiences. It offers an exploration of virtues that goes beyond conventional teachings, offering readers a deep, nuanced understanding of their role in spiritual growth.

The crafting of the Catechism was a testament to Father Francisco Palau's meticulous and thoughtful approach to Christian education. He did not merely opt for an encyclopedic collection of Christian doctrine; instead, he chose to focus on elements with immediate practical applications to everyday life, creating a practical guide to Christian living.

Given the wide breadth of Christian doctrine, it was an impossibility to cover all areas comprehensively within the scope of 52 Lessons, hence a selection had to be made. The methodology adopted by Father Francisco was shaped by this reality. He prioritized vital, concrete matters over theoretical and transcendental ones, following the philosophical traditions of St. Thomas Aquinas. His dedication to practicality was an acknowledgment of the dynamic nature of faith, which required an understanding and application that evolved with the changing times and pastoral needs.

Father Francisco's Catechism revolved around the principles of human behavior and the practice of virtues. He recognized that one's moral compass is determined not just by the understanding of divine word but also by reason. This served as a guiding principle in his teachings - a Christian's actions should reflect the teachings of their faith in a logical and responsible manner. The Catechism, therefore, served a dual purpose: it provided religious instructions and also fostered responsible citizens, further emphasizing the role of faith in societal harmony.

The contents of the Catechism were divided into three major sections, focusing on virtue in general, virtues in partic-

profound writings of ascetical and mystical authors, and even the insights of the solitary hermits – all serve as invaluable guides on this path.

As the teachings on virtue grow vast, it becomes essential to have a compendium that simplifies and distills the doctrine to its core principles. These principles, once grasped, serve as the foundation, shedding light on the teachings and fostering a clear, simple understanding of virtue. Such compendiums are often presented in the form of catechisms.

The Catechism, then, as per Palau's vision, would cover the breadth of virtue – its nature, its various types, the gifts of the Holy Spirit, the interconnection of all virtues, their relationship with the gifts of the Holy Spirit, the source of virtues, their growth and progression, and their application based on individual state and vocation. Every virtue identified by the Ecclesiastical Doctors would be examined, exploring their object, acts, and opposing vices.

The Catechism would be divided into Lessons, with each Lesson being a topic of discussion. The aim would be to facilitate the teaching of this science, referred to as the science of saints, in a systematic and comprehensive manner. As the Book of Wisdom [10,10] states, "God has given man, the science of the saints," serving as an eternal beacon guiding the School of Virtue on its divine mission.

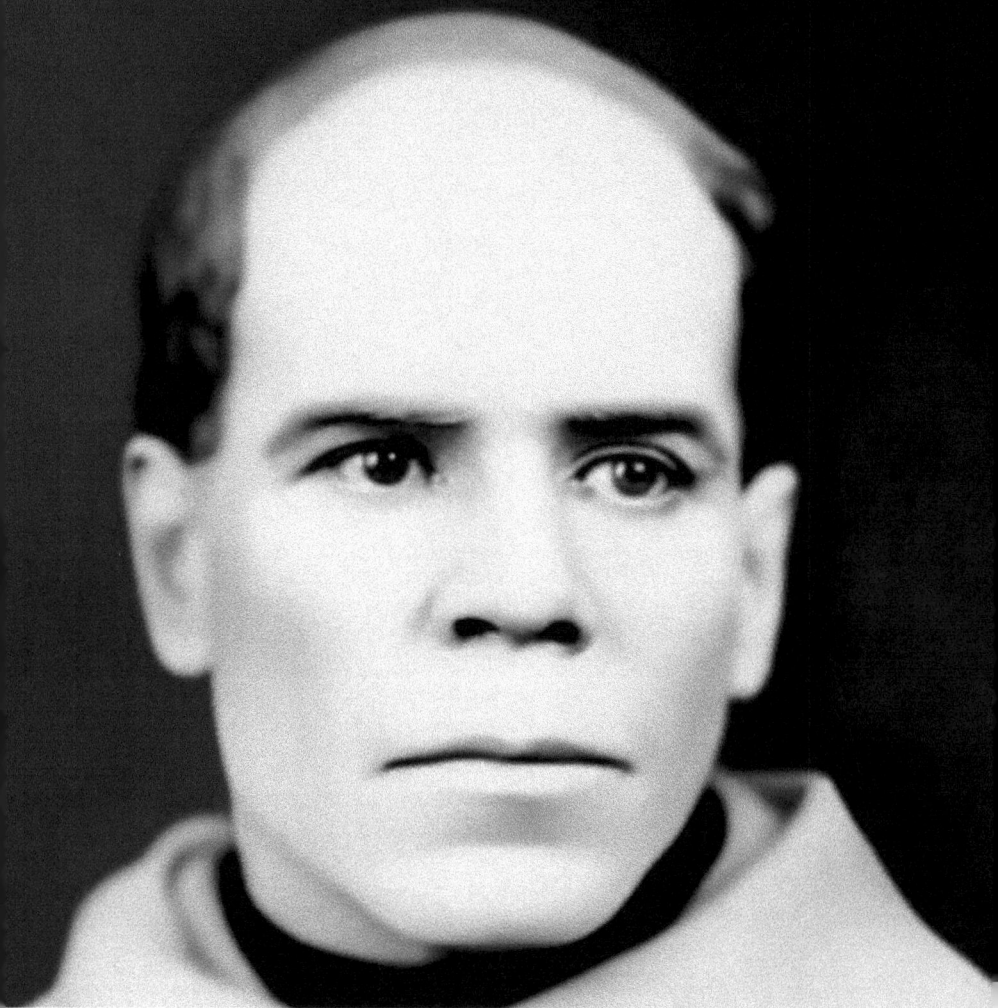

First Section: School of Virtue

Lesson 1: True Happiness

Q: What is happiness?

A: Happiness is a perfect state that encompasses all goods.

Q: How many ways can happiness be considered?

A: There is objective happiness, formal happiness, perfect happiness, imperfect happiness, natural happiness, and supernatural happiness.

Q: What does objective happiness consist of?

A: It consists of that which makes us happy.

Q: What does formal happiness consist of?

A: It consists of the act by which one possesses or attains the aforementioned object.

Q: What is the object that can make a person happy?

A: God alone.

Q: How is God possessed?

A: Through vision, comprehension, and enjoyment in glory: this is perfect happiness.

Q: By what means does a person in this life progress, attain, and unite with the object of their happiness?

A: Through virtue: this is imperfect happiness.

Q: What is natural happiness?

For His mercy has been confirmed upon us, and the truth

Q. How many fruits of the Holy Spirit are there?

A. Many, but they can all be grouped into twelve primary ones, which are charity, joy, peace, patience, kindness, goodness, long-suffering, gentleness, faith, modesty, self-control, and chastity.

Lesson 4: Connection, Order, and Harmony

Q: Is there a connection between virtues, and the gifts and fruits of the Holy Spirit?

A: Yes, there is a connection.

Q: Where does this connection come from?

A: This connection comes from the unity of the object that they all focus on.

Q: What is this object?

A: This object is to guide humans to their ultimate purpose and unite them with God, the source of their happiness.

Q: Can you present this connection with a simile?

A: Yes. Just as the roots, trunk, branches, leaves, and fruits form a single plant with the sap flowing through it, in the tree of virtue, charity is the trunk, habits are the roots, acts are the branches and leaves, and the most perfect aspect of the acts is the fruit of perfection. Our heart is the garden, grace is the rain that waters the plant, and the gifts are the sap that rises through the roots, gathers in the trunk, and divides, circulating and filtering through all the branches, leaves, and fruits.

Q: According to this simile, are all virtues united in one, which is charity?

A: Yes, they are.

Q: Do intellectual virtues maintain any order among themselves?

A: Yes, all intellectual virtues are united in wisdom.

Q: What about moral virtues?

A: The same applies; all moral virtues are interconnected and united in prudence.

Q: Can infused virtues, gifts, and fruits be present in a person who does not possess charity?

A: Not in a perfect way, but they can be present imperfectly.

Q: Can moral and intellectual virtues exist without charity?

A: Yes, because they are natural virtues.

Q: Can faith and hope exist in a person without charity?

A: Not as perfect virtues, but they can exist as imperfect virtues.

Q: If virtues and the gifts of the Holy Spirit are united and form a single entity, do we all need to have them all?

A: No, there are specific virtues for different states, which should be possessed and practiced only by the individuals in those states. However, we should all be prepared to practice these virtues if circumstances require us to do so.

Q: What is the source of the multitude and variety of virtues?

A: The source of the multitude and variety of virtues lies in the different objects they are directed towards.

Lesson 5: Seed of Virtue

Q. Where does virtue come from?

A. From God. He is the Lord of Virtues.

Q. What is the seed of natural virtues?

A. These have their beginnings in the synderesis.

Q. Where do supernatural virtues come from?

A. From the Holy Spirit, who infuses them into our heart. God sows both types of virtues—natural virtues as the author of nature, and supernatural virtues as the author of a supernatural order.

Q. Where does God plant this seed?

A. In the garden of our soul.

Q. In which part of our soul does virtue take root?

A. In the higher part, that is, in our understanding and in our will. The tendency of intellectual powers towards truth and the inclinations of the appetitive powers towards good make our soul a garden capable and suitable to receive the seed of all virtues.

Q. Can this same garden also receive the seed of vices?

A. Yes, because our understanding can receive light and dark, truth and error; and our will, being free, can choose to embrace either good or evil.

Q. Why is it that some people are more suited to one virtue

Lesson 10: Virtue Consists in a Just Middle

Q. What is the object of virtue?

A. A challenging, difficult, but attainable good.

Q. Why is this good challenging and difficult?

A. Because it has excesses to avoid and defects to correct, difficulties and obstacles to overcome.

Q. Does virtue consist of a middle ground?

A. Yes. Just as the perfection of a thing consists in its compliance with its rule and measure, the goodness of human acts lies in their compliance with their rule and measure.

Q. What is the middle ground of moral virtues?

A. The right reason of man.

Q. What is the middle ground of intellectual virtues?

A. The same as that of moral virtues, with the difference that the rightness of reason is the middle ground of intellectual virtues, and the rectified reason is that of moral virtues.

Q. Do theological virtues also have a middle ground?

A. Yes. Since God is the object that regulates them, there is no excess on this part, and where there is no excess, there is no middle ground because it lies between defect and excess; they have a middle ground on our part. Each person must go to God, believing, hoping, and loving according to their condition, state, or degree of perfection. In this, there can be excess and defect.

Q. Can we see the middle ground of virtues through some comparison?

A. Yes. There is one that is quite fitting. The holy city of Jerusalem is built on the highest and most sublime of all mountains; virtue is what leads us to it. Original sin opened chasms, cliffs, and abysses on all sides, such as the darkness of understanding, the malice of the will, the concupiscence of the flesh, the weakness of the heart to do good, and the violence of passions for evil. Virtue is the path, with cliffs of excess and defect on both the right and left; falling into fire or water, falling into the abyss of a defect or the pit of an excess, all of it is falling.

Lesson 11: Precepts given on the practice of virtues

Q. Is man obligated to strive for perfection?

A. Yes. God decreed in His wisdom not to give man all his perfection in the first instant of his creation. The time that Divine Providence grants him life on earth is ordered so that he can obtain his perfection in and with it. He is born extremely imperfect. And since in the holy city of glory nothing enters that is not perfect, he must use his time, strength, and actions to perfect himself in this life.

Q. If man is obligated to strive for perfection, and virtues are what accomplish this work in him, is he also obligated to practice them?

A. Negative and affirmative precepts have been imposed on us regarding the practice of virtues.

Q. What are the negative precepts?

A. Those that prohibit a wrongful act, such as "You shall not kill" [Dt 5,17].

Q. What are the affirmative precepts?

A. Those that command a good act, like loving God for who He is - that is, infinite goodness - and loving your neighbor as yourself [Lv 19, 18; Mk 12,30-31; Rm 13,8-10]. Negative precepts are imposed against vices and affirmative precepts regarding the exercise of virtues.

Q. How and when do these precepts obligate?

Ria Christie Collections

Marketplace: abebooks.com
Markt Order #: 692655593
Order Date: 2024-11-06

Order #: RCCL59121

Please dispatch to:
Yvette Khoury
131 Magdalen Road
Oxford OX4 1RJ
United Kingdom

Sender/ Return Address:
Ria Christie Collections,
Suite B; ARUN House, ARUN
Building, Arundel Road,
Uxbridge, Middlesex, UB8 2RP,
UK

Qty	Item	SKU	Price
1	The Catechism of Virtues:...	ria9798399716572_Isuk	GBP 8.49

Total Weight: 205.48g

Shipping: GBP 0.00
VAT: 0.00
Total: GBP 8.49

Notes:

Thank you for placing your order with us. Need help? Get In touch
with us via ryefieldholdings@hotmail.com.
YOUR 5* FEEDBACK IS ALWAYS APPRECIATED

A. Negative precepts always oblige and in every circumstance. It will never be allowed to lie, steal, or blaspheme.

Q. When do affirmative precepts oblige?

A. These do not always oblige, but rather depend on the circumstances.

Q. Is man obligated to practice all virtues?

A. There are virtues that are common to all classes, all states, conditions, and occupations, such as faith, hope, charity, prudence, justice, fortitude, and temperance; others are specific and characteristic of a state. We are obligated to practice virtues, each according to their position, strength, state, and occupation.

Q. When and on what occasions should virtues be practiced?

A. Not always, but when circumstances require it. If a vice attacks a virtue, such as impurity attacking chastity, there is an obligation to perform acts of virtue. If there are dangers of falling into a fault, we are obligated to prepare our hearts to preserve them from it, which is done through acts of virtue.

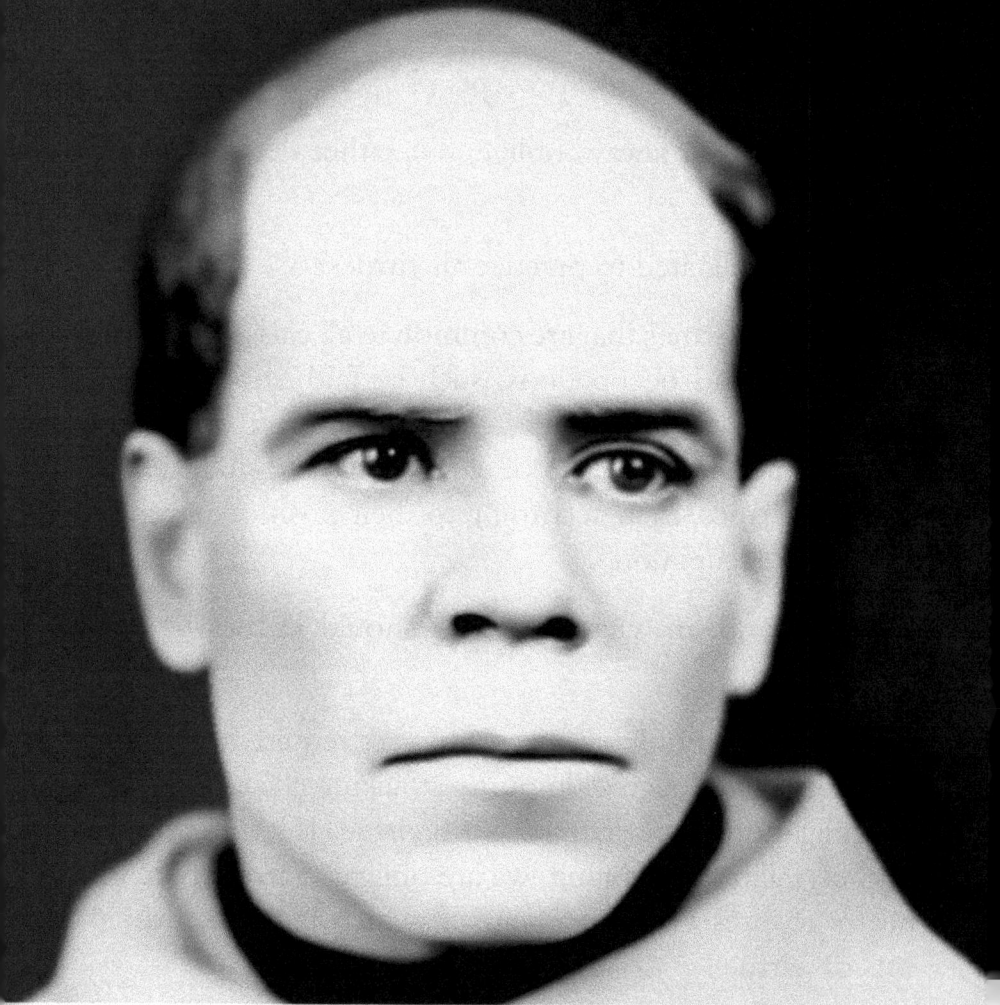

Section Two: Virtue Considered in Particular

Lesson 12: Exploration of Intellectual Virtues

We have already discussed virtues in general; now let's examine each of them in particular. First, we will look at the natural virtues, and then the supernatural ones. We have already mentioned that natural virtues rectify human beings in relation to their natural goals and are subdivided into intellectual and moral virtues; let's examine the intellectual virtues first.

Q. What is an intellectual virtue?

A. It is a habit that perfects and rectifies human reason and prepares one for good actions in relation to their natural happiness.

Q. How many intellectual virtues are there, and what are they?

A. There are five: wisdom, understanding or intelligence, knowledge, prudence, and art.

Q. What is the purpose of all these virtues?

A. To rectify human reason and regulate the noblest of their operations, which is reasoning.

Q. What is intelligence?

A. It is a habit that rectifies human reason in the consideration of everything that is known by itself. What is known by itself should be regarded as the principle of everything we can naturally know.

Q. What is wisdom?

A. It is a habit that perfects a person in the consideration of the highest, universal, and general causes.

Q. What is knowledge?

A. It is a habit that rectifies human reason in the understanding of particular and less principal causes. These three virtues rectify speculative reason. Prudence and art rectify practical reason.

Q. What is prudence?

A. As an intellectual virtue, it is a habit that rectifies human practical reason in relation to everything that is achievable, that is, in relation to all human actions.

Q. What is art?

A. It is a habit that rectifies human practical reason in relation to everything that is feasible, such as building houses, constructing machines, etc.

Q. How many arts are there?

A. Some are liberal, and others are mechanical; liberal arts are those that involve more mental effort than physical, such as grammar, rhetoric, geometry, painting, arithmetic, geography, and others. Mechanical arts require more physical labor than mental, such as agriculture, machinery, and others.

Q. Why is art a virtue?

A. Because it rectifies human practical reason and enables one to perform good actions well. Let's consider a practical example: cultivating the land is a naturally good activity, agricultural rules provide guidance and instruction for doing everything related to this art well. Agriculture perfects humanity in this aspect and, in relation to this objective, this art is a natural virtue.

For His mercy has been confirmed upon us, and the truth

Lesson 13: Moral Virtues

Q. What is a moral virtue?

A. A moral virtue is a habit that rectifies and disposes all of a person's faculties to follow the right dictate of reason. The purpose and object of all moral virtues is to help people live according to the right dictate of reason.

Q. How many moral virtues are there?

A. As we have mentioned before, there are many moral virtues, but they can all be reduced to four cardinal or principal virtues: prudence, justice, fortitude, and temperance. Let's discuss prudence.

Q. What is prudence?

A. As a moral virtue, prudence is a habit that rectifies the dictate of reason concerning all human actions.

Q. What is the difference between prudence as a moral virtue and prudence as an intellectual virtue?

A. As an intellectual virtue, prudence rectifies a person's practical reason in relation to all human actions. As a moral virtue, it rectifies the dictate of that reason and makes good use of it by ordering what should be practiced, how, and in what manner, in all specific cases.

Q. What is the object of prudence?

A. To rectify the dictate of reason.

Q. How many and what are its acts?

A. There are three acts of prudence: 1) to deliberate, ponder, seek, and discover what is appropriate to do in all specific cases; 2) to judge what is most useful and suitable for the circumstances based on the findings; and 3) to command the implementation of what has been found most useful and judged most conducive to the intended goal.

Q. Which is the principal act of prudence?

A. The principal act is the right dictate or the command.

Q. If prudence is a cardinal virtue, or one that has many other virtues related to it, which are these virtues?

A. The virtues associated with the four principal virtues can be considered as parts of them: some as integral or essential parts, others as potential parts, and others as less principal virtues subject to the cardinal virtue.

Lesson 14: Integral Parts of Prudence

Q. How many virtues are there that are considered integral or essential parts of prudence, and what are they?

A. There are eight: memory, reason, intelligence, docility, diligence, foresight, circumspection, and caution.

Q. Since these eight virtues are integral parts of prudence, is there any harmony and connection between them?

A. Yes. They all focus on a single goal, which is to strengthen the guidance of reason. We have already mentioned that three acts are necessary for the correct guidance of reason: seeking what should be done, judging what is most useful among the options found, and commanding the execution of what is considered most appropriate for the intended purpose.

To strengthen the first act, the following serve: 1) the memory of everything past; 2) the knowledge of everything present, whether from contingent or necessary causes; 3) the docility in seeking advice from others; 4) the diligence or eustochia, which consists in finding prompt and easy means proportionate to the goal proposed by reason. Through the past and present, and through what others have told or advised us, we infer what should be done in the future and in specific cases.

For the second act, reason or reasoning serves. By reflecting on all the means presented to us and comparing them with each other, we judge which option is the most direct and suited for the particular case.

For reason to command the execution of the means found to be most useful and judged most appropriate, three things are necessary: 1) that everything ordered is adapted to the proposed purpose; 2) foresight serves for this; 3) that, in execution, attention is paid to the circumstances of the matter, and this is achieved by circumspection. Finally, the obstacles are overcome, difficulties are dealt with, and impediments are conquered that may arise in the execution of the means found, proposed, and judged most appropriate for the intended goal.

Q. How many and what are the parts of prudence that the angelic teacher Saint Thomas Aquinas calls subjective parts?

A. These are virtues subject to the principal or cardinal virtue, different in nature from each other. Under this consideration, the subjective parts of prudence are: 1) individual prudence, which governs an individual; 2) social prudence, which governs a group. This is subdivided into military, economic, regnant, and political. Military prudence directs an army in battle, economic prudence organizes families, regnant prudence guides a ruler, and political prudence governs subjects in a city, kingdom, or empire.

Q. How many and what are the virtues related to the cardinal virtue of prudence called potential virtues?

A. These are virtues that perfect the main virtue in certain secondary acts and matters that do not have the full essence of virtue. Prudence has three such virtues: eubolia, synesis, and gnome.

Q. What are these three virtues?

A. Eubolia rectifies a person and helps them give good advice; synesis assists in rectifying one's judgment in everything they should do in particular cases; gnome is distinguished from synesis in that the latter judges according to ordinary and common rules of prudence, while the former, in certain unforeseen and particular cases that are beyond the reach of common rules, judges according to higher principles and governs prudence by superior rules.

Lesson 15: Vices Opposed to Prudence

Q. What are the vices opposed to prudence?

A. As with all other moral virtues, prudence is opposed by some vices due to excess, and others due to deficiency. The vices of deficiency against prudence are: imprudence, rashness, recklessness, thoughtlessness, inconstancy, and negligence.

One can be imprudent due to malice, by disregarding the rules of prudence, or due to negligence, by failing to practice them for the success of the matter at hand. If one moves forward with a matter without first seeking good advice about it, there is rashness. There is thoughtlessness if one does not look for or disregards everything that can help refine their judgment on what should be done. Rashness lacks good advice; thoughtlessness lacks right judgment; and inconstancy either fails to execute what has been deemed appropriate or abandons the action halfway through the endeavor.

Q. Is negligence a vice that sins due to deficiency against prudence?

A. Yes. Negligence opposes prudence either due to contempt for the rules prescribed by this virtue for the success of all matters or due to a lack of proper diligence in seeking good advice and forming the right judgment about what needs to be done.

Q. What vices oppose prudence due to excess?

Lesson 16: Justice

Q. What is justice?

A. Justice is a habit by which one willingly and consistently gives to each what is due to them.

Q. Is justice a virtue?

A. Yes, because it makes the one who possesses it just.

Q. Where is the middle ground of the moral virtue of justice?

A. In a certain equality of proportion between the external thing and the person; between more and less. The middle ground is equality.

Q. What is the main act of justice?

A. To give each one what is due to them.

Q. Is judgment an act of justice?

A. If it is right, it is an act of justice. To be right, it must conform to the nature of the thing. Doubtful matters should be interpreted favorably. One should not judge a person as bad based on mere suspicions.

Q. What are the parts of justice?

A. There are three: the subjective, the quasi-integral, and the potential or related virtues.

Subjective Parts

Q. What are the subjective parts of justice?

A. Distributive justice and commutative justice.

Q. What is distributive justice?

A. It involves giving each party what is due based on their merit.

Q. What is commutative justice?

A. It is giving to each what belongs to them.

Q. Is restitution an act of commutative justice?

A. Yes.

Q. What is restitution?

A. Returning to the owner what has been stolen or what is being withheld against their will.

Q. Is restitution of stolen goods necessary for salvation?

A. Yes.

Q. What are the vices opposed to this subjective part of justice?

A. The vices opposed to distributive justice are favoritism or partiality.

Q. What is this vice?

A. It consists of giving gifts not based on the merit of the recipient but for other reasons, such as friendship, kinship, or recommendation.

Q. What are the vices opposed to commutative justice?

A. All those that cause harm to our neighbors. We can

harm our neighbors in their persons or their possessions, through actions or words.

Homicide, mutilation, flogging, imprisonment, exile, theft, and robbery are vices opposed to this virtue by excess. There are also vices in judgments: on the part of the judge when pronouncing a sentence; the accuser presenting untrue facts; witnesses not telling the truth; the defendant in their defense; and the lawyer in their advocacy. Insults, defamation, slander, mockery, and curses are also contrary to commutative justice, whose damages must be repaired.

Q. What are the vices committed in contracts?

A. Deceit and fraud are found in buying and selling.

Q. In which contract is usury committed?

A. In lending.

Q. What is this vice?

A. It consists of demanding and taking something for the favor done to the one who receives it.

Q. Is there any title that authorizes the lender to demand something for the loan?

A. Yes. This can only be done when there is lucrum cessans and damnum emergens; that is, when the loan causes the lender some real and true harm or deprives them of an actual profit.

Q. How many quasi-integral or essential parts of this cardinal virtue are there and what are they?

A. Two: to avoid evil and to do good.

Q. What vices are there against these two parts?

A. Two: those caused by sins, one of transgression, and the others of omission.

is in God, who with His grace, the gifts of the Holy Spirit, and infused virtues, moves, prepares, and disposes our hearts and makes them agile and ready in the matters of His service.

Prayer

Q: What is prayer?

A: The lifting of our soul to God; or better yet, an internal act inspired by religion, through which a person asks God for graces, recognizing Him as the author of all good things.

Q: In how many ways can prayer be considered?

A: In two ways: mental and vocal.

Q: What is mental prayer?

A: It is the prayer made in the spirit without the noise of words.

Q: What is vocal prayer?

A: It is asking God for favors with our voice.

Q: As prayer is an intimate, friendly, and familiar conversation between a person and their God, have ascetic and mystical Doctors taught any method or rule that can guide us in learning this conversation?

A: The saints have left us such good books about prayer that there is nothing better we could desire. As prayer is an exercise that is so significant for the practice of all virtues, we will briefly and concisely summarize the most interesting aspects of this subject within the scope of a catechism.

Lesson 19: The Parts of Prayer

The exercises of prayer have been divided by ascetic and mystical doctors into seven main points called the parts of prayer, which are: preparation, reading, meditation or contemplation, petition, offering, thanksgiving, and summary or epilogue. Let us examine each of these parts.

Q: What does the preparation consist of?

A: There is a remote and proximate preparation. The remote preparation consists of not forgetting God in our daily affairs, always being vigilant of ourselves. The proximate preparation is what is done in prayer, which includes the following acts: 1) awareness of God's presence; 2) examination of conscience; 3) an act of reconciliation with God through an act of contrition.

Q: What is the purpose of meditation?

A: Reconciled with God through contrition, we choose the subject of meditation. In the morning, this could be the life, passion, and death of Jesus, and in the evening, the last things. Having chosen the subject of meditation, we ponder upon it, and our thoughts and meditations aim to form purposes and resolutions to serve God with greater perfection; to strengthen our heart to pursue the good it has decided upon; or to attack vices, practice virtues in a specific way; and to imitate Jesus Christ and certain saints in what suits our position best.

Q: Is meditation the same as contemplation?

A: No. Meditation is an act of understanding that focuses on material objects represented in our imagination. We make reflections and observations by comparing and combining different things. Contemplation is a simple act of understanding where our spirit focuses its intellectual eye on a truth without speculation or combination. Contemplation reaps the fruit of meditation, as our understanding, tired of pondering, rests and focuses on a truth that interests it more.

Q: When should we meditate and when should we contemplate?

A: It is difficult to give a general rule for this. If our understanding cannot ponder and meditate, we should propose an object in whose simple presence it can gather and rest. Such is the presence of God.

Q: What, when, and how should we ask of God?

A: The petition is a part of prayer. We ask God for the common good of the Church, or for the living or the dead, those graces we need for our temporal and eternal happiness.

Q: Can we ask for material goods?

A: We can ask for them, but only as secondary or directed to eternal goods.

Q: What conditions are necessary for a petition to be a meritorious and impetratory act of religion?

A: Four conditions are necessary: 1) believing in God's promises; 2) trusting in His goodness; 3) not putting any obstacle on our part with faults and sins; 4) making ourselves, through our actions, worthy of what we ask for, doing what we know and can to deserve the graces we request.

Q. Can someone in mortal sin ask God for grace?

A. Yes, but the first thing they should ask for is help to escape from sin and do their part to reconcile with God.

Q. When should we ask God for favors?

A. In all our needs, especially when we find ourselves in imminent danger of falling into mortal sin.

Q. In how many ways can prayers be directed to God?

A. In secret, in public, alone or with others, with the spirit or with the voice.

Q. What is an offering?

A. It is a part of prayer. Our own faults can hinder the supplications we present for ourselves, and public scandals can hinder the ones we make for the common good. Against these obstacles, we offer to the Father the prayers that Jesus his Son addressed to him while he lived on Earth. We offer his Son as a sacrifice to appease him, as a pure and immaculate host for the satisfaction of our debts, and as an inestimable and infinite price to redeem us from the slavery of passions, the world, and the devil. We offer his merits against our demerits. We can also offer him the prayers of his Most Holy Mother and of all the saints and all their merits.

Q. What is thanksgiving?

A. It is a part of prayer in which, after having meditated and recognized God as the author of all the good things we have or will ever have, we give him thanks as a sign of gratitude for having received them from his hand.

Q. What is an epilogue?

A. The conclusion of this important exercise. The epilogue contains an examination of the conscience regarding the way the prayer has been carried out. A compilation of all the affections is made, as well as all the intentions and resolutions taken. By keeping them in mind throughout the day, they can be put into practice at the appropriate times.

Q. How much time should be spent in prayer?

A. This depends on the nature of one's business, the position of the individuals, and their state and duties.

Q. How should people practice prayer in the aforementioned seven parts?

A. It is not necessary to always follow this order; they can engage in one part or another at times, depending on the movement of the spirit.

Lesson 20: External Acts of Religion

Q. How many and what are the external acts of religion?

A. There are three. First, there are the acts of latria, through which a person, with bodily movements, shows and gives God the veneration, honor, submission, and respect that is due to Him. Second, there are those acts through which we give and offer God something external. Lastly, there are other acts by which we invoke the name of God and use it for a good, holy, and praiseworthy purpose.

Q. Regarding the first, what is adoration?

A. Adoration is an external act of religion by which a person gives God the reverence, respect and signs of submission that are owed to Him.

Q. What are these signs or bodily acts or ceremonies called?

A. The worship of religion.

Q. What is the worship given to God called?

A. Latria.

Q. Can we worship saints?

A. Yes, but only insofar as they are friends of God, our intercessors, and under the consideration that God's glory and virtue shines and radiates through them.

Q. What is the worship we give them publicly called?

A. Dulia. And the worship given to the Mother of God, the Virgin Mary, is called hyperdulia.

Q. Coming to the second, what external offerings do we give to God, and for what purpose?

A. Concerning this, there are sacrifices, oblations, first fruits, and tithes.

Q. What is a sacrifice?

A. A religious act by which a victim is offered to the Supreme Being in acknowledgment of His absolute dominion over all things and in sign of our submission to His will.

Q. What did the sacrifices of the old law represent?

A. The true Lamb, which is Jesus Christ, who was sacrificed on the altar of the cross and is daily offered to the Father on our altars.

Q. What is an oblation?

A. An offering made to God of temporal goods, in sign that we have received all things from His hand.

Q. What are first fruits?

A. The first part gathered from the fruits of the earth, offered to God as a sign of gratitude.

Q. What are tithes?

A. The tenth part of the products offered to and given to God, for the maintenance of the priests, the support of the churches' worship, or to aid the needs of the poor.

Q. When and for what purpose do we invoke the name of

God?

A. Concerning this, there are vows, oaths, and the praises of God.

Q. What is a vow?

A. A promise made to God with an obligation to do or give something that is pleasing to Him.

Q. How many kinds of vows are there?

A. Simple and solemn vows, conditional and absolute, perpetual or temporary.

Q. In what does the solemnity of the vow consist?

A. In a person's commitment to God and the acceptance by the Church.

Q. What is an oath?

A. Taking God as a witness to some action.

Q. Is it lawful to swear?

A. Yes, as long as the proper conditions are observed, because it is an act of religion.

Q. What is a conjuration?

A. Invoking the holy name of God to bind Him to do what we ask, desire, or command.

Q. Is using the name of God for praising Him an act of religion?

A. Yes.

Lesson 21: Vices Opposed to Religion as a Moral Virtue

Q: Is religion, being a moral virtue attached to the cardinal virtue of justice, in a balance between excess and defect, having vices on both sides?

A: Yes, as with all the other virtues.

Q: What is its balance?

A: The proper worship of the Divine.

Q: Where are the vices that attack it?

A: Superstition opposes it by excess and irreligion by defect.

Superstition and Its Types

Q: What is superstition?

A: A vice opposed to religion in which a person worships the true God in an inappropriate manner or gives to creatures the worship that is due to God alone.

Q: How many types of superstition are there?

A: Four: worshiping the true God in a wrong way, idolatry, divination, and vain observances.

Q: Regarding the first, where is the superstition?

A: It can arise either from the reality represented in the ceremonies or from the person giving the worship. There would be superstition if someone used ceremonies to signify things that are fantastical and not real, such as portraying Christ as though he were still to come and suffer. In this sense, the worship that Jews give to God is superstition. Superstition can also arise on the part of the ministers of worship, such as when they represent the mysteries of religion with ceremonies and rites not approved by the Church or with different ones than those the Church is accustomed to using.

Q: What is idolatry?

A: Giving worship to a creature that is due to God alone.

Q: What is divination?

A: Predicting future events in an illicit and improper manner.

Q: In how many ways can divination be illicit?

A: Four: 1) consulting demons, the dead, or magnetized persons to know something; 2) looking at stars and their movements to know future contingents or the future actions and fortune of people; 3) relying on dreams; and finally, 4) paying attention to the songs and other movements of animals.

Q: What are vain observances?

A: Using certain signs or words to know contingent future events or to gain an inheritance, fortune, or similar things, which signs have no relation to the thing signified.

Q: How many and which are the vices opposed to the virtue of religion by defect?

A: Four: tempting God, perjury, sacrilege, and simony.

Q: When and where is it said to tempt God?

A: When one relies on divine help while at the same time being negligent and careless in doing everything within one's power to avoid evils and dangers and to obtain the graces requested.

Q: What is perjury?

A: Taking the name of God to swear to a statement or fact that is false, or a lie confirmed by an oath.

Q: What is sacrilege?

A: The desecration, violation, or any irreverence concerning sacred things or persons. Everything that is dedicated or intended for divine service, whether things, persons, or places, is sacred.

Q: What is simony?

A: A tacit or explicit contract by which spiritual things, or things related to them, are bought or sold.

Q: Can the Church and its ministers make contracts with the people regarding adequate and suitable sustenance for their rank?

A: Yes, because those who serve the people have a right to demand what is suitable and necessary for their subsistence.

Q: Can the clergy and the people make agreements and contracts about each act of ministry?

A: No, but the clergy can accept alms given to them in gratitude for the charity they exercise with the people.

Lesson 22: Piety

Q. What is meant by "piety" in this context?

A. A virtue related to justice, by which parents and the homeland are given the respect and honor that is due to them.

Q. What is meant by "parents" in this context?

A. It refers not only to the father and mother, but also to all other blood relatives and family members. And under the term "homeland," it includes all fellow citizens and friends of the same country.

The virtues of piety and religion may seem to be in opposition.

Q. Should acts of religion be abandoned in order to serve parents?

A. If religion calls us to its aid, and parents, relatives, fellow citizens, and friends put obstacles in our way, giving in to their demands would no longer be an act of piety, but a formal disobedience to God. If piety calls us to assist our parents, and we turn a deaf ear to their voice and go to non-obligatory acts of religion, this religion would no longer be a virtue, but a vice. In practice, circumstances and the position of individuals should be considered.

Q. What vices are there against this virtue?

A. One sins against it by excess, when they show their parents signs of hatred, enmity, or insult through actions, words, or gestures. And by deficiency, when they fail to show respect and love at the appropriate times or do not help them in their needs.

Observance

Q. What is observance?

A. A virtue related to justice, by which we give those in positions of dignity the honor and respect that is due to them.

Q. What is meant by "persons in positions of dignity" in this context?

A. It refers to both ecclesiastical and civil authorities, their governments, and all persons who represent them.

Q. What vices does this virtue oppose?

A. By excess, one sins against justice when they insult a person in a position of dignity. By deficiency, when they fail to show honor and respect at appropriate times.

Q. Are "dulia" (veneration) and obedience parts of observance?

A. Yes, because dulia gives superiors the honor and respect that is due to them, and obedience provides the proper submission to their authority.

Lesson 23: Obedience

Q. What is obedience?

A. Obedience is a virtue connected to religion, through which we submit to our superiors as is due, to each one within the sphere of their jurisdiction.

Q. Should we obey God in all things?

A. Yes, because He is the sovereign, the Lord, and the universal ruler of all creatures.

Q. Should we obey people vested with dignity and authority?

A. Yes.

Q. In everything, to everyone, without any restriction?

A. No. That would be disorderly.

Q. What shall we obey them in?

A. To each of them, within the sphere of their respective authority.

As a human being, we are subject only to God, the author of nature, and we are free within the scope of our natural actions. As Christians, we are subject to the prelates of the Church in the territory defined by ecclesiastical laws. As citizens, we are subject to civil authority within the limits established by civil laws. As a servant (if in service), we are subject to our masters according to the laws of the contract. If a member of the military, we are subject to our respective superiors within the scope of authority defined by the rules of discipline. As a child (if still a minor), we are subject to our parents in all matters relating to family life. As a religious person (if having taken vows), we are subject to the prelates of the order within the jurisdiction granted by the monastic rules or constitutions. As a penitent, we are subject to our confessor in the tribunal of penance in all matters necessary for the integrity of the confession and the validity of the sacrament.

Q. Is obedience a virtue?

A. Yes, because it makes a person good, that is, obedient to their respective superiors; by giving them the due obedience, we demonstrate justice, as obedience is a virtue connected to justice.

Q. If obedience is one of the moral virtues, where is the defect, the mean, and the excess?

A. It has disobedience as its defect.

Q. Is disobedience a sin against justice and religion?

A. Yes, because giving due obedience to superiors is an act of justice as well as an act of religion, and denying it is an injustice.

Q. What vices does obedience have as an excess? Is it a sin to be too obedient?

A. It can be, and it is: 1) when the superior commands against God or His law, or commands evil things; 2) when the commands go against the orders of the 3rd Rule: We shouldn't obey our superiors if our voluntary obedience would lead us towards a harmful and perverse end.

Q: Is the person who obeys on a safe path?

A: The obedient one, as an obedient person, cannot be lost. Since obedience is a virtue, obeying is walking on a safe path. However, this applies to obedience given to superiors as a virtue attached to religion and the potential of justice. In voluntary obedience, we can easily deceive ourselves and be deceived. Voluntary obedience is the one we give to people outside the circle of authority. Within this circle, obedience is an act of religion and justice. Outside of it, it is merely a free act of our will, through which we humbly follow the advice of another person. Freely following the advice of another person is called direction. In matters concerning our spiritual well-being, this obedience is called the direction of souls. There can be direction in other areas as well: in a legal case, the lawyer directs the cause they defend; a leader directs their company in battles; a priest can guide souls with their advice and doctrine towards the path of perfection.

Q: What kind of obedience does a person need to follow the path of their perfection by their director (or guide)?

A: In terms of justice, none since obedience is voluntary and direction is based on advice. However, if a superior directs the subjects within the territory of their jurisdiction, obedience would be justifiable.

Q: Are the confessor and director the same thing?

A: No. The confessor is a superior in the sense that they are a judge sitting in the seat of conscience to judge the cause of the penitent. Rigorous and just obedience is owed to them in matters of conscience, i.e., confession. The director doesn't have any other authority than the one voluntarily given by those who follow their advice.

Q: What qualities should obedience have to be perfect, when considered as a virtue attached to justice?

A: 1) It should be blind regarding what is ordered;

2) It should be prompt in executing the commands;

3) It should be humble, subjecting one's judgment and will to the superior;

4) It should be faithful, not interpreting the command in a distorted way, according to the tacit or presumed will of the superior;

5) It should be voluntary, not expressing complaints against the superior;

6) It should be joyful, finding glory, pleasure, and happiness in serving their God and Lord, represented by the superior.

Q: If obedience should be blind, could a madman lead us to perdition?

A: As a moral virtue, obedience is blind; it's not its role to examine whether the person giving the orders is a legitimate superior, whether their commands are good, or whether it is appropriate to obey. This is the role of prudence. Prudence has eyes; it must examine whether it is right to obey or not. However, the other virtues guided by prudence are blind and should follow its judgment.

Lesson 24: Gratitude, Revenge, and Truth

Q. What is gratitude?

A. It is a virtue related to justice, by which we give our benefactors their due reward, whether it is by saying thank you, through our actions, or in any other way.

Q. What are the acts of this virtue?

A. 1. Recognizing the benefit received; 2. Giving thanks to the benefactor; and 3. Repaying them according to the time, circumstances, place, and qualities of the person.

Q. Is ingratitude a sin?

A. It is a vice against justice and religion, and therefore, a sin.

Q. Are we obligated to give thanks to God for the benefits received from His hand?

A. Yes, because He is our primary benefactor.

Q. When should we give thanks to God?

A. Every time we receive a special benefit from Him. We should also give thanks after eating, and occasionally for the benefits of creation, preservation, and redemption, which are the main ones.

Q. What is revenge?

A. A virtue related to justice, by which punishment is imposed on the lawbreaker proportionate to their offense, to promote their amendment and safeguard the common good.

Q. Is revenge allowed?

A. When carried out by someone with authority and in the proper way, it is a virtue.

Q. In what way is truth a potential virtue of justice?

A. It means that a person should present themselves in deeds and words before others as they truly are in themselves and before God.

Q. What vices are opposed to truth?

A. Lying, pretense or hypocrisy, and boasting.

Q. What is lying?

A. Speaking words contrary to what one thinks, with the intent and desire to deceive.

Q. How many types of lies are there?

A. There are malicious lies, humorous lies, and white lies. The first is harmful, the second serves our neighbors' benefit, and the last is told to please others and ourselves.

Q. Is lying a sin?

A. It is always a sin and can never be allowed in any case. The truth may be withheld, but lying will never be permissible.

Q. What is pretense or hypocrisy?

A. Pretense is appearing outwardly different from what

one truly is. Hypocrisy involves pretending to be a different person than one actually is, such as appearing righteous while being wicked.

Q. What is worse, being a hypocrite or causing scandal?

A. Causing scandal. The hypocrite ruins only themselves, while scandal harms both its cause and others. There may be a case when the hypocrite is worse: when they pose as a sheep to prey on others [Matthew 7:15]. In this case, it is better that the wolf be discovered than passed off as a sheep.

Q. Should a wicked person present themselves as they truly are in front of others?

A. If they are a hidden sinner, they would be adding the sin of scandal to their own. It is terrible to be wicked, but it is worse to proclaim it, and boasting about it would be intolerable. The hypocrite should present themselves before God and in their conscience as they want to appear before others, but not vice versa.

Q. What is boasting?

A. Making oneself appear greater than they truly are through words, signs, or actions.

Q. What is irony?

A. Presenting oneself as lesser than they really are. This can happen in two ways: 1. Preserving the truth by remaining silent about one's virtues, which is not a sin; 2. Committed falsely and with vice by declaring untruthfully low qualities about oneself or denying significant qualities that one knows they possess.

Lesson 25: Affability, Generosity, and Equity or Epikeia

Q: What is friendship or affability?

A: Affability is a virtue related to justice, through which a person behaves in a decent and appropriate manner in conversation and communication with others.

Q: What are the opposing vices?

A: The opposing vices are flattery and quarrelsomeness.

Flattery is a vice where, in conversation, a person seeks to please and delight others, even when it may be more appropriate to cause distress. While affability involves behaving in a courteous manner in conversation with others, it does not prevent us from distressing others when necessary to prevent some harm or promote some good. Flattery occurs when one tells another pleasant but false things with the intention of causing spiritual or physical harm. Flattery is also a fault when the adulator's praise causes harm to a third party, either with malice and intention or unintentionally.

Quarrelsomeness, on the other hand, is a vice in which a person causes distress to others without necessity.

On Generosity

Q: What is generosity?

A: Generosity is a moral virtue related to justice, through which we make good use of the things that Providence has entrusted to us for our sustenance. This virtue has two vices to avoid: extravagance attacks it by excess, and greed by deficiency.

Q: What is greed?

A: Greed is the disordered desire to possess earthly goods.

Q: Is it a capital vice?

A: Yes, because many other vices stem from it.

Q: What are these vices?

A: They include betrayal, deception, lying, perjury, restlessness, violence, oppression of the poor, and stubbornness in works of mercy, etc.

Q: What is extravagance?

A: Extravagance is a vice in which a person lacks the proper care and attention required in managing the wealth and fortune that Providence has given them for their own or their family's maintenance or abuses it through false administration by giving more than their position allows.

On Epikeia or Equity

Q: What is epikeia?

A: Epikeia is a virtue related to justice, which, in uncommon and extraordinary situations, follows the intention of the legislator rather than the law, because applying the law would cause serious harm, both to the individual or to the community for which it was given.

Q: Is following the law in cases not anticipated by the legislator, to the grave detriment of the individual or the community, a sin?

A: Yes, it is against equity or epikeia and against justice.

Lesson 26: Courage

Courage is one of the four cardinal virtues. We will discuss this moral virtue in three main points: First, we will ask what this virtue is and then we will see what its parts are.

Q. First, is courage a virtue?

A. Yes, because it makes the person who has it good and makes all their actions good.

Q. How does courage make a person good?

A. Every human virtue consists in living according to reason. This can be achieved in three ways: 1°. In that reason itself is rectified, which is done by prudence and the other intellectual virtues; 2°. In that this rectitude is applied to human affairs, which is done by justice; 3°. In that obstacles are overcome and impediments are avoided that may arise against this rectitude, which is done by courage and temperance.

To live according to reason, a person encounters two types of impediments. One arises from the will and appetite, which are drawn, driven, and moved by earthly goods, delightful and pleasurable temptations, to another end contrary to right reason. Against this obstacle, the will and appetite are ordered by temperance. Another impediment exists in us to follow the correct dictate of reason, and it is: the most horrible evils that must be endured, hardships that must be borne, obstacles that must be overcome; on this side, courage rectifies and orders the spirit, and under this consideration, it is a virtue.

Q. According to what has been said, what is courage?

A. One of the four cardinal virtues that makes a person firm and constant in following the dictate of reason against all obstacles and impediments that may be presented to them.

Q. What are the main acts of courage?

A. To endure and to attack. To uphold the order proposed by reason in human actions against obstacles. To break through inconveniences. To destroy the impediments that exist against the order proposed by right reason in human actions.

Q. Is martyrdom an act of courage?

A. Yes. It is to endure, even to suffer the greatest of all evils which is death, the order proposed by right reason or faith in human actions.

Q. How many things are necessary for martyrdom?

A. Three: to suffer death; that this death is given in hatred of religion or to uphold virtue, and the state of grace on the part of the martyr.

Q. What are the vices contrary to courage?

A. By deficiency, it has fear or timidity, and by excess, it has recklessness or fearlessness.

Q. What is timidity?

A. A shrinking of spirit in the presence of evils that right reason dictates should be endured and suffered.

Q. What is fearlessness?

A. Not fearing where there is real danger.

Q. What is recklessness?

A. A passion that attacks evils that should be tolerated, or if they should be overcome and destroyed, combats them in an inappropriate way.

Lesson 28: Magnanimity and Magnificence

Q. What is magnanimity?

A. Magnanimity is a virtue, an integral part of fortitude, which strengthens and makes our hearts firm to follow the right judgment of reason, despite facing the most serious dangers that may arise.

Q. Is magnanimity a virtue?

A. Yes, it is.

Q. If it is a virtue, what are its extremes and defects?

A. Its excesses are presumption, ambition, and vanity; its defect is pusillanimity. To understand these vices, we must note that a person on the path of virtue faces grave dangers to avoid and fear. These dangers include the honors, dignities, and the worldly possessions that can draw our hearts away from virtue, as well as death, sufferings, torture, exile, imprisonment, hunger, poverty, etc., which can weaken our spirits and discourage us from continuing on the virtuous path.

Presumption is a vice by which a person undertakes objectives that exceed their ability and strength. While the magnanimous person aspires to great, difficult, and hard-to-obtain goals, they do not exceed the means adopted for achieving them.

Q. What is ambition?

A. Ambition is a vice opposed by excess to magnanimity because it leads a person to excessively desire and attach themselves to honors. The magnanimous person does not desire honors they do not have; and if given, they offer and attribute them to God, to whom all honor and glory is due, without becoming attached to them.

Q. What is vainglory?

A. Vainglory is a vice opposed by excess to magnanimity, in which a person places their affection and happiness in their own glory or disordered appetites for glory in things not deserving of it. The magnanimous person does not desire acclaim that they do not have and is not attached to the acclaim they do have, offering it instead to God.

Q. Is vainglory a capital vice?

A. Yes, because it gives rise to many other vices, such as disobedience, boasting, hypocrisy, contention, obstinacy, discord, and the presumptuous invention of novelties, according to St. Thomas Aquinas.

Q. What is pusillanimity?

A. Pusillanimity is a vice opposed to magnanimity by deficiency, in which a person becomes discouraged and disheartened when facing the dangers they must overcome to pursue the good proposed by right reason.

The presumptuous person sins by attempting difficult virtues through means that exceed their capabilities and strength. The pusillanimous person sins either by believing they are incapable and unworthy of what is proportional to their strength or by giving up the effort to obtain the difficult. The magnanimous person believes they can achieve anything with God and nothing without Him. With their abilities and God's help, they believe they can achieve their ultimate goal, facing dangers and obstacles without fear.

Q. What is magnificence?

A. Magnificence is a moral virtue of fortitude, by which a person carries out, with great breadth and splendor of soul, everything they have set out to do in the most grand, sublime, and excellent way.

Q. What is the difference between magnanimity and magnificence?

A. Magnanimity strengthens the spirit for the greatest moral good, while magnificence is about achieving the greatest value, quality, and dignity in the realm of manmade things.

Q. What vices are opposed to this virtue?

A. The vices opposed to magnificence are parvificence and waste.

Q. What are these vices?

A. Parvificence is a vice in which a person undertakes and performs actions less grand than they could and should. Waste is a vice in which a person spends disproportionately or inappropriately for the work they intend to undertake or is already in progress.

Lesson 29: Patience and Perseverance

Q. What is patience?

A. Patience is a comprehensive moral virtue of fortitude, which strengthens the spirit to endure hardships and contradictions with tranquility and without disturbance in the practice of virtue.

Q. What are the acts of patience?

A. 1. To maintain a calm spirit in the face of suffering; 2. To not express discontent externally with words or gestures; 3. To protect the heart against sorrow, which is said to kill the soul; 4. To endure hardships with equanimity, stillness, and peace of mind, but also with joy, as it is a privilege to suffer for the name of God.

Q. What are the vices opposed to patience?

A. Restlessness, sadness, impatience, and anger.

Perseverance

Q. What is perseverance?

A. Perseverance is a moral virtue of fortitude, through which we steadfastly, firmly, and peacefully endure all hardships presented to us for the sake of virtue, even if they persist until the end of our lives.

Q. Is constancy a virtue of fortitude?

A. Yes, constancy is a part of perseverance and is a virtue

that strengthens the spirit in the pursuit of the good that we have aimed for.

Q. What are the vices opposed to perseverance?

A. Indolence and obstinacy.

Q. What is indolence?

A. Indolence is a vice opposed to perseverance, by which a person easily yields to evil and ceases to do the good they initially aimed for. Indolence can be caused by sadness due to the absence of delight or by difficulties encountered in the practice of virtue.

Q. What is obstinacy?

A. Obstinate is a vice by which a person persists in their resolutions, endeavors, and actions for longer than dictated by right reason. An indolent person gives up too easily, while a persevering individual upholds the good and endures the evil for as long as right reason dictates.

Lesson 30: Temperance

Q. What is temperance?

A. It is one of the four cardinal virtues, which strengthens a person and prepares them to follow the right judgment of reason against the desires of the flesh.

Q. What is the object of this virtue?

A. To moderate the pleasures of the flesh, the main ones being touch and taste.

Q. Where does the balance, deficiency, and excess lie?

A. The balance consists of using pleasures according to the needs of life, which are: propagation of the species in terms of touch, and individual preservation in terms of taste. Insensibility is the deficiency, and intemperance is the excess.

Q. What is insensibility?

A. Rejecting those pleasures that are necessary for the propagation of the species and the preservation of the individual.

Q. What is intemperance?

A. It is a disorderly appetite for pleasure, or a vice by which a person desires and craves those pleasures that are not in accordance with, against, or prohibited by reason and law.

Q. Temperance, being a cardinal virtue, undoubtedly has many other moral virtues in its retinue. Let us see what these are.

A. Temperance, like all other cardinal virtues, has integral, subjective, and potential parts. The integral parts are: shame or modesty and sincerity.

The subjective aspects are: abstinence and sobriety, chastity and purity.

The virtues related to the main virtue are: continence, humility, gentleness or clemency, modesty, good order, adornment, austerity, frugality, and simplicity.

Quasi-integral parts

Q. What is sincerity?

A. It is a quasi-integral virtue of temperance by which a person loves everything that is worthy of honor.

Shame or modesty is a virtue by which we abhor, detest, avoid, and fear everything that is worthy of disgrace, infamy, and dishonor.

Lesson 31: Abstinence and Sobriety

Q. What is abstinence?

A. Abstinence is a moral virtue of temperance that directs a person's desires for the pleasures of taste arising from food.

Q. What is fasting?

A. Fasting is the voluntary deprivation of a portion of food that is not necessary for the preservation of life.

Q. What is ecclesiastical fasting?

A. Ecclesiastical fasting is the deprivation of a portion of food not necessary for an individual's well-being, according to the rules prescribed by the Church.

Q. Is fasting an act of abstinence?

A. Yes, it is, because it corrects the disordered appetite for food.

Q. What are the vices opposed to abstinence?

A. Gluttony.

Q. What is gluttony?

A. Gluttony involves five aspects: eating at inappropriate times, extravagantly, in excessive quantities, with intense desire, and seeking with eagerness, care, and study delicate and delicious things.

Q. Is it one of the seven capital vices?

A. Yes, because it encourages, causes, and gives rise to many others.

Q. What are these?

A. Gluttony, according to the angelic teacher St. Thomas Aquinas (Question 148, Article 6), has five daughters: the joy of fools or senseless people, buffoonery, uncleanness, gossip, and mental dullness.

Sobriety

Q. What is sobriety?

A. Sobriety is a moral virtue of temperance that moderates a person's appetite for drink.

Q. What is the vice opposed to sobriety?

A. Drunkenness.

Q. What is this vice?

A. A disordered appetite for drinks.

Q. How can a person exceed with this vice?

A. In the same ways as they can with food: by drinking at inappropriate times, extravagantly, in excessive quantities, with intense desire until one loses their judgement, and by seeking with care and eagerness the most precious and exquisite beverages.

Lesson 32: Chastity and Virginity

Q. What is chastity?

A. Chastity is a subjective virtue of temperance that moderates and regulates venereal pleasures.

Q. How many types of chastity are there?

A. There are three: conjugal, widowed, and virginal. Conjugal chastity is for married people. Widowed chastity is for widows, and virginal chastity is for virgins.

Q. What is modesty?

A. Modesty is a virtue that moderates and regulates human touch, appearance, and venereal acts.

Q. What is virginity?

A. Virginity is a subjective virtue of temperance and related to chastity, by which a person preserves, consecrates, and devotes their physical and spiritual integrity to their Creator against any venereal acts, whether licit or illicit. Alternatively, it is a firm resolution to keep one's body and spirit pure from any venereal acts, whether licit or illicit.

Q. What are the vices contrary to chastity?

A. Lust and its varieties.

Q. Is lust a capital vice?

A. Yes, it is because it leads to many other vices.

A. Against meekness, there is wrath, and against clemency, there is cruelty.

Q. What is wrath?

A. An disordered appetite for revenge.

Q. Is it a capital vice?

A. Yes, because it leads to many others, such as: quarrels, inflated pride, insult, loud outbursts and shouting, indignation, and blasphemy.

Q. What is cruelty?

A. A harshness of mind in imposing penalties; severity and ferocity are related to cruelty.

Q. What is modesty?

A. Modesty is a moral virtue associated with temperance that moderates a person's outward actions.

Modesty moderates four aspects: the inclination or movement of the mind towards some excellence, which it does through humility; the desire for knowledge, which it moderates through studiousness, opposing curiosity; everything pertaining to external actions and the movement of our body so that they are done decently, both that which is done seriously and what is done in jest; And lastly, everything related to the outward appearance, such as bodily gestures, clothing, and similar things.

According to this, modesty is a virtue that contains others, which are humility, studiousness, and the sense of proper behavior.

Lesson 34: Humility, Studiousness, and Eutrapelia

Q. What is humility?

A. It is a moral virtue related to temperance and joined to modesty, which moderates and rectifies the disordered appetite for one's own excellence.

Q. What acts does this virtue have?

A. St. Anselm (Book of Similitudes, chapters 99 to 108) notes the following: 1. To consider oneself as something despicable. 2. To feel pain for being so. 3. To confess oneself as such. 4. To persuade others to believe it. 5. To patiently endure others telling it. 6. To suffer being treated as such. 7. To love contempt or being despised; and, if one reaches the point of rejoicing in being despised for the sake of virtue, this will be the highest degree of humility.

Q. Is magnanimity perhaps a virtue opposed to humility?

A. No. Humans, in what they have from God, elevate themselves, become magnanimous, and aspire to obtain everything they believe they can achieve and possess through their virtues and God's gifts. This is magnanimity. In what they have of themselves, they humble themselves and, believing themselves incapable of doing good and capable of committing any evil, they despise and regard themselves as nothing. This is humility.

Q. What vice is against humility?

A. Pride.

Q. What is pride?

A. A disordered love for excellence or for high and great things of which one is incapable.

Q. In how many ways does one sin through pride?

A. 1. Believing that the gifts one has are from oneself; 2. If one believes they have them from above, thinking they were given because of their merits; 3. Boasting of having what they do not have; 4. Despising others, as it seems to them that they alone possess what they have.

Q. Is it a capital vice?

A. It is not only a capital vice but the principal one of them all. Pride is the queen (says St. Gregory in the XXXI Moralia) of all vices. After having completely taken over a person's heart, it surrenders them to the other six as six chiefs, who, with all the other vices, finish devastating and disordering it. From these springs the infinity of all the other vices that corrupt one to the point of obstinacy.

Q. What is studiousness?

A. It is a virtue, related to temperance and joined to modesty, that moderates the inclination and the appetite for everything pertaining to the knowledge of truth.

Q. What vice is against it?

A. Its opposite vice is curiosity, which is a disordered appetite for knowing or learning.

Q. What is eutrapelia?

A. A virtue that moderates a person in games.

Q. Are there any other virtues related to modesty that moderate a person in their external gestures and movements, and in the dressing and adornment of the body?

A. There are two: the adornment of the body, and the decency and good ordering of all movements and external acts. These virtues moderate a person in dances and performances.

Lesson 35: Precepts on the practice of moral virtues

Q. The entire law is contained explicitly or implicitly in the precepts of the Decalogue. Where can we find those pertaining to prudence?

A. In all the precepts of the Decalogue, since prudence is the directive of all virtuous acts commanded by the law. If the precepts are given to us regarding virtuous acts, how much more so for prudence, which directs them!

Q. Where are the precepts concerning justice?

A. The ten precepts explicitly speak about justice. The first three command the acts of religion; the fourth, piety; and the other six command or prohibit acts concerning justice in general.

Justice imposes duties that the law commands us to fulfill. These duties are with God, with other people, and with ourselves. The first three precepts command us to fulfill our duties to God; we owe Him love, and for this reason, we are told: "You shall love your God with all your heart, with all your soul, and with all your strength" [Dt 6:5; 10:12; Mt 22:37]. In the second precept, we are forbidden to take His holy name in vain through oaths, blasphemies, and curses. The third precept commands that we give Him public and private worship on holidays, as is due to Him as the living and true God. The fourth precept says to respect, honor, and pay attention to our parents, relatives, and fellow citizens as they deserve. And in the other six precepts, we are commanded to fulfill the remaining duties we have to our fellow human beings and are prohibited from theft, fraud, deception, murder, lies, usury, abduction, and other vices that cause harm to others.

Q. Where are the precepts pertaining to fortitude?

A. These are implicitly contained in the entire Decalogue. It commands us to perform virtuous acts and prohibits vicious ones. In order to practice virtue and avoid vices, fortitude is necessary. Its acts are commanded in all the precepts given to us concerning virtue. Both the Old and New Testaments have given us explanations on this: "Do not fear them," we read in Deuteronomy, "for the Lord our God is with us [Dt 7:21]. Take up God's armor," writes the Apostle to the Ephesians, "and stand firm and strong against the devil's schemes" [Eph 6:11].

Q. Is there an explicit precept in the Decalogue about temperance and all the other virtues associated with it?

A. In the sixth precept, all forms of lust are forbidden, which is one of the seven deadly sins contrary to temperance. The acts of this virtue and all the virtues associated with it are implicitly commanded in all the precepts of the Decalogue. The reason is this: in the law, we are commanded to practice all virtues, which cannot be done without properly resisting all the suggestions of concupiscence, which are restrained by temperance and its associated virtues.

Lesson 36: Supernatural Virtues

We have already seen what natural virtues are. Now we will talk about supernatural virtues.

Q. What is a supernatural virtue?

A. A habit infused into the soul that perfects a person in order to achieve their ultimate end.

Q. What is the ultimate end of a person?

A. As we have mentioned in the first Lesson, only God can be the object of happiness and therefore, the ultimate end.

Q. According to this, does the supernatural virtues perfect a person in all relationships they have or can and should have with God?

A. Undoubtedly.

Q. How many are the supernatural, divine, or theological virtues?

A. As we have said previously, there are three: faith, hope, and charity.

Q. Why are they called theological or divine and supernatural?

A. They are called theological because they direct all human actions and operations towards God, whether internal or external, and order everything in our hearts according to Him. They are called divine because only God infuses them. They are supernatural because we cannot know them with our own understanding, and even if we could, we could not possess them with our own strength alone.

Let's see what they are.

Faith

Q. What is faith?

A. A habit infused into the soul by which we believe the revealed truths that the Church proposes to us as such. Or, it is a habit infused into the soul, which is the principle of everything we hope for and through which our understanding is convinced to believe what we do not see.

Q. What is the object of faith?

A. Revealed truth.

Q. Are the truths that we know naturally the object of our faith?

A. What we know naturally, we see. And what we see, we do not believe. Therefore, the object of our faith can only be revealed truth.

Q. What is revelation?

A. Knowledge of everything that we know only because God has told us.

Q. Is revelation possible?

A. Yes, because it would be foolish and lacking common sense to think that God cannot speak to people.

Q. Is revelation a positive fact? Has God spoken to people?

A. Yes.

Q. To whom, how, and when?

A. People should not only be considered as solitary individuals, but also as members of a community, with a social nature. When associated with others, they form a perfect moral body. If we consider a person as an individual, God, as the author of nature, speaks to their heart from the throne of their conscience. He dictates what one must do and avoid in order to achieve natural happiness, and reveals the natural law, saying deep within their heart: Do good and avoid evil. Treat others as you would want to be treated. Do not kill. Do not steal. Worship your God, etc. [Tb 4:15; Mt 7:12; Lc 6:31; Ps 34:15]. God, the author of natural order, continuously speaks to people. People respond, make excuses, defend themselves, and condemn themselves. To deny this would be foolishness.

When considered as part of a moral body, people hear the voice of God through all those who are in positions of political and religious authority. God, as the author of natural order, dictates what society needs to know for its temporal and eternal happiness.

Q. I believe this because it does not require great proof. What I ask is: has God revealed things to people that are beyond their reach and which people or nation has He directed His word to?

A. The Catholic, Apostolic, Roman Church is the depository of the word of God; that is why we have said that faith is believing in the revealed truths presented by the Catholic, Apostolic, Roman Church.

Q. I want to know what the Church is, how and when God

has spoken to it, what He has said, and whether or not it is infallible in what it proposes for us to believe.

A. Let's save this for the following Lesson.

Lesson 37: The Church of God

Q. What is the Church?

A. Church means assembly. If this assembly consists of evil people, it is a malignant church; if it is made up of spirits gathered to give due worship to the living and true God, it is the Church of God. In this sense, there is a triumphant Church, a purgative Church, and a militant Church.

Q. What is the triumphant Church?

A. It is the assembly of the predestined who give due worship to God in glory and in the proper way.

Q. What is the purgative Church?

A. It is the assembly of souls who give due worship to God in purgatory.

Q. Do the souls in purgatory worship God?

A. There is no doubt. They are His friends and adore, glorify, and reverence Him in the way their painful position allows.

Q. What is the militant Church?

A. It is the assembly of people who give due worship to the living and true God on earth in the proper way.

Q. Tell me something about the Catholicism of the Roman Church and the revelation it proposes to us.

A. All the peoples who give the true God the worship He is due belong to it. This people were born with Adam and from Adam. In paradise, God spoke to our first parents, and after their sin, He promised them a Redeemer. He spoke to all the patriarchs who worshipped Him with their families according to the particular forms inspired in them. When the children of Adam were abandoned to the disorder of their passions, a flood of water covered the earth, and only Noah and his family were saved in the ark, a symbol of the true Church. The children of Noah, having been corrupted by the abominations of idolatry, God chose a special people: Abraham and all his descendants. God spoke to Abraham, Isaac, and Jacob. He spoke to the twelve tribes of Jacob, giving them His written word. This written word, the Holy Scripture, was faithfully preserved until the coming of the promised Messiah. The Roman Church, founded by Jesus Christ and His apostles, received this Scripture intact, incorrupt and unaltered, and guards it as the most precious of all treasures. God spoke to people through His own Son. He spoke through the apostles. The Holy Spirit spoke to them and speaks through the mouths of holy Fathers and Doctors.

Q. How can it be proven that this Holy Scripture is the true word of God?

A. Those who announced it proved their mission with all the signs and divine evidence necessary to convince a person who can reason and who does not want to blind themselves in the face of the truth. The divinity of the Scriptures presented to us by the Roman Catholic Church is proven in a way that is capable of convincing and persuading every sensible person of sound judgment.

Q. How is the existence of the Patriarchs, Prophets, and

Apostles; the existence of a Messiah; and all the facts related to them in these divine books proven?

A. By tradition. How do we know that Alexander the Great, Aristotle, Cicero, and Napoleon Bonaparte existed? Who has transmitted their deeds to us? Tradition. Similarly, tradition proves the existence of the Patriarchs, Moses, the Prophets, Jesus Christ, the Apostles, Church Fathers and Doctors, and the truthfulness of all their actions.

Q. Is the Roman Catholic Church infallible when proposing what God has or has not revealed, what must be believed and what must not be believed?

A. Yes, it is. It would cease to be the people of God and His true Church if it could err in this regard.

Q. To whom does the task of examining whether a truth is revealed or not belong?

A. Although any individual can do this examination, the right belongs to the Church.

Q. To whom does the authority to define, decide, and resolve what is revealed truth by God and what is not belong?

A. This is a prerogative of the true Church.

Q. Whose responsibility is it to propose what must be believed and what must not be believed?

A. The Roman Catholic, Apostolic Church.

Q. Are we obliged to believe everything that God has revealed to us?

A. Yes, because God is infallible truth that cannot be mistaken or deceive.

Q. Are we obligated to believe as a matter of faith everything that the Church proposes to us as something revealed?

A. Yes, the opposite is heresy.

Q. When we are not sufficiently sure whether something is revealed or not, what should we do?

A. We should seek information about whether the Church has defined it as a matter of faith or not.

Q. Is doubt in this case a sin?

A. No, because it is not against faith.

Q. Once we are sure that the Church has defined something as a matter of faith, are we allowed to doubt whether it is revealed truth or not?

A. No. Doubt in this case would be heresy.

Lesson 38: Articles of Faith

Now that we have seen what the Church is and its infallibility, it is important for us to know what must be believed and what must not be believed, and what God has said and revealed to people.

Q. Is everything contained in the books that make up the Holy Bible to be believed as revelation?

A. Not only this, but also everything that the Catholic, Apostolic, Roman Church has defined as a matter of faith.

Q. Can our beliefs be summarized in a compendium?

A. Yes. The Apostles compiled everything in the Creed. The Catechisms of Christian Doctrine are a summary of everything that a good Catholic is obliged to believe.

Q. I would like to have a more explicit version of the Creed. Could everything be reduced to a few points or articles?

A. Yes. Here are the articles of faith, to which we will add everything that disbelief attacks in our day.

The statement that the Apostles compiled the Creed should not be taken literally. It was made in the Church based on their preaching. The Creed proposed here, corresponding to the traditional formula of the catechisms, is called the Nicene-Constantinopolitan, as it was drafted at the ecumenical councils of Nicaea (325) and Constantinople (381).

1. Believe in one almighty God, creator of heaven and earth.

2. Believe that He is the Father. 3. That He is the Son.

4. That He is the Holy Spirit.

5. That the Father, Son, and Holy Spirit are three distinct persons and one true God.

6. That He is the Redeemer.

7. That He is the rewarder of the good and the punisher of the wicked.

These belong to the Divinity. Those concerning the Humanity of Jesus Christ are as follows:

1. Believe that the second person of the Holy Trinity, the Son, took flesh in the purest womb of the Blessed Virgin Mary, the legitimate spouse of Joseph, descendant of the royal family of David, and originally from the tribe of Judah.

2. That He was born of the Blessed Virgin Mary, who remained a virgin during childbirth, before childbirth, and after childbirth.

3. That He was arrested, judged, and sentenced to death under the power of Pontius Pilate, with Caiaphas as the high priest.

4. That He was crucified and voluntarily suffered the most horrible and shameful death to save the world, and was buried.

5. That He rose from the dead on the third day after being crucified.

6. That He ascended to heaven and sits at the right hand of God the Father.

7. That from there, He will come to judge the living and the

who have authority. 2) As soon as a person reaches the age of reason. 3) Whenever temptations become so strong that they put a person in imminent danger of succumbing. 4) If God's holy name is insulted by Christians with blasphemies and impieties, those who are firm must confess their faith so that the weak, ignorant, and vulnerable do not falter. 5) Whenever it is required by the honor due to God and the necessity or usefulness to the faithful.

Another act of faith is never denying it, and this, at the cost of our lives and any other sacrifice.

Q. What are the effects that faith produces in true believers?

A. 1) Faith directs our intellectual gaze to its own object, which is God, eternal truth, and, assisted by the gifts of the Holy Spirit, purifies the understanding of all errors it has in relation to Divinity, its ultimate end and all that leads to it; 2) it infuses holy fear, because it presents God as supreme goodness and as the rewarder of the good and the punisher of the wicked.

Q. In what way is faith a supernatural infused virtue?

A. 1) Because the truths that are presented to us far exceed the capabilities of natural light; 2) it is infused by the Holy Spirit because without its gifts, the human heart would not consent to believe, and the intellect would not captivate its natural thinking nor be convinced or overwhelmed.

Q. Are the mysteries of our holy faith contrary to reason?

A. No. On the contrary, they are very much in line with it.

The fact that human beings cannot penetrate the mysteries

that faith proposes with their own light is not against reason; just as it is not against reason that there are secrets in nature that we cannot fathom with our own light.

Q. How can people consent to believe in things they do not know and cannot know, and that are obscure to them?

A. Obscurity is a property of faith because we believe only in what we do not see or know. If we saw it, we would not believe it. Faith presupposes the existence of a supreme intelligence whose sight extends to infinitely knowable objects, whose understanding, being of infinite virtue, knows truths that are mysteries and secrets to all other inferior intelligences. If we believed only in what we see and know with our own light, we would deny the existence of other intelligences superior to humans. If these exist, what is clear to them is obscure to us, what they see and know, we believe because they have told us. This is faith.

Lesson 40: Vices Contrary to Faith

Q. Does faith consist of a just medium?

A. In terms of its object, faith has no excess, and therefore, it has no medium. However, there is a medium on our part. In this consideration, the medium consists of neither being overly credulous nor incredulous but believing in what God has revealed to us, as proposed by the Church, our Mother.

Q. Where is the defect and where is the excess?

A. Denying God what is fitting is sinning by defect. Attributing to God what is unfitting is sinning by excess. Believing in something as revelation when it is not, or believing in something as revealed when it does not have all the characteristics of true revelation, is the excess of foolish credulity. Believing easily without examining whether what is proposed to us has all the characteristics of divine revelation is exposing oneself to illusions and deception.

Q. What vices does faith have by defect?

A. There is only one that includes many others, and it is unbelief, which consists of failing to believe in what is proposed to us as revealed by those authorized to propose it to us.

Q. How many vices does unbelief contain?

A. They are almost innumerable, but they can be reduced to a specific number, which are atheism, deism, paganism,

Judaism, Protestantism, heresy, apostasy, and blasphemy.

Q. What is atheism?

A. Denying the existence of God, and attributing everything to matter and chance.

Q. Who are the deists?

A. Those who accept the existence of a God, recognize Him as the author of the natural order, but deny revelation.

Q. What is paganism?

A. Some people have never been exposed to the Gospel, leading to material paganism. Others have heard the message but resist it, leading to formal unbelief.

Q. What is Judaism?

A. This error consists of denying the coming of the Messiah and believing that the one promised by the prophets is yet to come.

Q. What is the main error of Protestants?

A. Not recognizing the Church of God as a visible moral body. From this stems the refusal to recognize the Roman pontiff as Christ's vicar and head of the Church. They deny all jurisdiction to prelates, adhere only to what their whims dictate, believe themselves capable of defining matters of faith, interpret Sacred Scripture as they wish, believe what they want, and deny what is inconvenient to them.

Q. What is heresy?

A. Heresy is the stubborn denial of any of the articles of

Lesson 41: Hope

Q. What is hope?

A. Hope is a supernatural virtue, infused in the soul, by which we hope to obtain blessedness with the help of Almighty God and our good deeds.

Q. What is the object of our hope?

A. There is a primary and secondary object. God, viewed as a good that can be obtained, is the main object of our hope. Accidental or accessory goods to essential glory are also objects of our hope.

Q. Can a man in a state of corrupted nature, with his own strength, come to possess God?

A. This is impossible. God is for man the greatest good, the only one capable of making him happy; but difficult and impossible to attain by our own strength. It is a supernatural end that is beyond the reach of all human efforts, totally exceeding all our natural virtues, and under this consideration it is impossible to obtain.

Q. On what do we base our hopes then?

A. In the help of Almighty God and in our good deeds. God, infinite goodness, will give us in this life the help of His grace, by which we will practice virtue and flee from vice. By practicing all virtues, we will become worthy of eternal glory; and being worthy of it, God, the just judge, will give it to us after this life.

Q. According to this, we hope for God's help in this life to serve Him, and in the other, eternal glory. What reasons do we have for hoping in this life for the assistance of grace to be able to do good, to practice virtue and avoid vice?

A. We have already said that faith was the foundation or principle of everything we hope to receive from God. Faith, therefore, presents to us God the Redeemer of men, and as infinite goodness, offers His friendship, His grace, His mercy, and forgiveness to every contrite and humbled sinner.

The help of grace, it is true, was lost through original sin, but Jesus merited it for us by His life, passion, and death. This help is promised to us by God. These promises have been given to us written in the sacred books. These Scriptures are signed with the finger of God and sealed with the blood of His only begotten Son. Our hopes are therefore founded on the omnipotence, goodness, wisdom, and faithfulness of God and on our good deeds.

Q. Is hope a virtue?

A. Yes. Because it presents to us God as an object, though difficult and hard to possess, yet possible; thus it moves us towards Him.

Q. In what is it a supernatural virtue?

A. Because only God can inspire it in the soul. It is a theological virtue because it looks to God as a good that can be obtained.

Q. Do the damned have hope?

A. They cannot have this virtue because they see God as an impossible object to possess. Impossible, because they lack the means which are good works and the help of grace.

Q. Do the souls in purgatory have this virtue?

A. They do have it because, for them, God is a supreme good that can be possessed over time. Possible, through the satisfaction of the penalties owed to their faults.

Q. Do the blessed have this virtue?

A. No, they don't have it because what is possessed is not hoped for.

Q. Can the hope of the pilgrim man come to assure him with metaphysical certainty of the objects he hopes for?

A. No. As long as man lives in mortal flesh, he should not and cannot be sure, but should work out his salvation in fear and trembling [Philippians 2:12].

Q. Can there be any signs to know if the pilgrim man will be saved or not?

A. There can be no certain signs. If there were any that could assure us, it would be virtue; but we see the virtuous turning into the vicious and vice versa. However, we can conjecture that the virtuous person, if he perseveres while walking the path and practicing the means, will attain his end. We can assure eternal life to the righteous if they do not stray from the path of virtue.

Lesson 42: Vices Opposed to Hope

Q. Does hope consist in a proper balance?

A. In terms of the object it looks to, it has no excess, and therefore, no balance. The more our hopes are based on the help of Almighty God and our good deeds, the better. On this side, there can be no excess. But there can be both deficiency and excess under another consideration.

Q. What vices are opposed to hope?

A. Despair and presumption.

Q. What is despair?

A. Despair is a vice opposed by deficiency to hope, in which the pilgrim man considers God as something difficult and impossible to obtain.

Q. Where does this vice come from?

A. It may arise from an error contrary to faith, or from a false opinion about God's goodness, mercy, and justice. If he denies God the attributes that belong to Him, like goodness and mercy, if he does not believe in the help of His grace and the forgiveness of sins, this despair is an effect produced by his unbelief. In this case, despair is guilty of the sin of unbelief. The man must correct his judgment by faith regarding God's goodness and mercy; once the cause is removed, the effect is removed. What is error in the understanding is sin in the will. Consenting to heresy that denies God's mercy is a sin that leads to the abyss of

125

despair. We can only hope for what we believe to be possible. If one does not believe in God's mercy, he cannot hope for it.

Not only speculative error can produce despair, but also practical error. The pilgrim man may believe all that our Holy Mother Church proposes to us and make a vicious application of the general principles of faith. He may have pure principles and become corrupt in the practice and application of them. The man may believe that God offers His grace, mercy, and forgiveness to every pilgrim man and cease to believe that God gives it to himself. Consenting to this practical error is the sin of despair. This sin may proceed from a purely practical error, and this is often found in mistaken and scrupulous consciences. If those who fall into this error do, on the other hand, do everything that human frailty allows them to do in the service of God, they must discard their error, and the effect will be stopped by removing the cause. Neither our own faults and miseries nor the most enormous sins are sufficient reason to despair of God's mercy. It is precisely because we are what we are, that is frail, weak, wretched, sinful, that God offers us His grace, forgiveness, and mercy. Our miseries are the steps that will lead us to God, the highest good. This error may also arise from a vicious and disorderly life. In this case, despair is also an effect of bad living; but even if life is vicious, the man can and should hope: 1st, God will give him His grace and forgiveness if he repents of his sins; 2nd, he can and should hope that by doing what human frailty permits, God will lend him His hand to subdue passions and escape from the abyss of guilt; 3rd, he can and should hope that after leaving his guilt with the help of Almighty God, serving Him in this life, he will possess Him in the next. A man can sin against all moral virtues, and yet not fall into the sin of despair. Although he has committed the most heinous sins, there is no good reason for him to put the seal on his disgrace by committing an even greater sin, which is to despair.

Lesson 43: Charity

Q. What is charity?

A. Charity is a supernatural virtue infused into the soul, through which we love God for being infinite goodness, and our neighbors as ourselves.

Q. Is charity a virtue?

A. Not only is it a virtue, but it is the queen of all virtues.

Q. What is the object of this virtue?

A. God, as the highest and infinite good, is the primary object. We ourselves and our neighbors are the secondary objects.

Q. Who are our neighbors?

A. All those who enjoy God in glory, or who have the possibility and capacity to possess Him.

Q. What order should be followed in charity?

A. We must first love God.

Q. What degrees are there in the love of God?

A. 1st. Loving Him for the fear of being punished by His justice; 2nd. As the object of our happiness, with the hope of possessing Him in glory. The first is servile love, the second is interested love. 3rd. As an infinitely lovable good in itself. This is pure and filial love.

Q. Is servile and interested love bad?

A. No, because it is love of God.

Q. After God, whom and in what order should we love?

A. We should first love ourselves.

Q. How is this love for ourselves understood?

A. God is the highest good, universal, and the principle from which all good proceeds. We must love God for being the highest good. We must love ourselves for what we are and have from God, and we must love our neighbors for the same reason, that is, for what they are and have from God.

Q. Should we love our body?

A. Yes, because it is created to participate, according to its capacity, with the soul in glory.

Q. Should we love it as much as our soul?

A. No. Our soul is a much nobler and more excellent part, has more of God, and for this reason we should love it more than the body.

Q. What does true love for the soul consist of?

A. In adorning it, enriching it, and dressing it in all virtues, and saving and purifying it from the ugliness of vice.

Q. What does love for our body consist of?

A. In subjecting it to the spirit, rectifying and moderating passions, and making it serve as an instrument for the exercise of all virtues.

Q. Is the mortification of the flesh, disciplines, vigils, abstinence, mortification of the senses, fasting, and other things that disgust the body contrary to charity?

A. If all this is ordered by prudence, it is truly loving the body. On the contrary, letting the body run wild like an untamed horse towards its own tastes and pleasures is to hate it and prepare it for eternal fire.

Q. What is meant by self-love or egoism?

A. Any love that is not ordered by the laws of charity.

Q. Should we love our neighbors more than ourselves?

A. No. "You shall love your neighbors as yourself," [Lev 19:18; Gal 5:14] says the law. Self-love is the rule and model for loving our neighbors. We love ourselves for what we are and have from God, and for the same reason we must love our neighbors.

Q. Is there an order in the love of our neighbors?

A. Yes. The more they have of God, the more lovable they are. That is why we must love the saints more than the living for this reason and among them, more to those with greater sanctity.

Q. Are there other special reasons that compel us to love some more than others?

A. Yes. Such reasons are: kinship, friendship, beneficence, and many others.

Q. Should a husband love his wife more, and the wife her husband more than their children and parents?

A. Yes, because they are one flesh.

Q. Should husbands and wives love their children more than their parents?

A. Yes, because the children come from them.

Q. Should a child love their father more than their mother?

A. According to the laws of kinship there should be no preference; but in other respects, one may love one more than the other.

Q. Should we love other relatives according to their degrees of kinship?

A. Yes.

Q. Should we love our friends?

A. Yes. The laws of friendship prescribe this.

Q. Should we love our benefactors with a preference over strangers?

A. Acts of kindness are a reason for special love.

Q. Is being a citizen and acquainted with someone a reason for special love?

A. Yes, because they are closer than others.

Q. Should we love our enemies?

A. In the same way as ourselves, because they are our neighbors. We should hate the evil in them and love what is of God; they have a soul and a body capable of enjoying one day with us in glory.

Q. What does the love of enemies require us to do?

Q. What is benevolence?

A. An act of charity by which we do good to our neighbors according to our ability.

Q. What order should be followed in acts of benevolence?

A. The same order that we have already proposed, discussing charity, because benevolence is an act of it.

Q. What is almsgiving?

A. An act of charity by which a person, moved by compassion, gives something to a needy person to relieve their need.

Q. Does almsgiving belong to mercy?

A. Yes. It is commanded by mercy as an inner act and by benevolence as an external act.

Q. Therefore, will almsgiving be an act ordered by charity through mercy and benevolence?

A. No doubt.

Q. How many types of almsgiving are there?

A. Two: corporal and spiritual.

Q. What are the corporal almsgivings and how many are there?

A. Seven: 1st. feeding the hungry; 2nd. giving drink to the thirsty; 3rd. clothing the naked; 4th. visiting the sick and imprisoned; 5th. harboring strangers; 6th. rescuing captives; 7th. burying the dead.

Q. How many and what are the spiritual almsgivings?

A. There are seven as well: 1st. teaching the ignorant; 2nd. giving good advice to those in need; 3rd. consoling the sad; 4th. correcting those who are wrong; 5th. forgiving the offenses of our neighbors; 6th. bearing with patience the adversities and weaknesses of others; 7th. praying for the living and the dead.

Q. Which are more important, the corporal or the spiritual almsgivings?

A. The spiritual ones, because they aid a person in their most noble and important part, which is the soul.

Lesson 45: Precepts Imposed Regarding Charity

Q. Has God given any commandment regarding charity?

A. There is one that contains all others. The entire law of the Gospel is enclosed in the commandment of love: "You shall love God and your neighbor as yourself" [Lv 19,18; Mt 22,39; Gal 5,14; Rm 13,9]; this is the whole perfection of humans.

Q. How and when is almsgiving required?

A. For this, we must consider the circumstances. The neighbor might be a stranger, a relative, or a benefactor. They could be in extreme need, serious need, or merely in need. The person giving alms might have more or less ability to help. They might only have the essentials, or, in addition to what is necessary, some surplus and savings. All these circumstances considered, they resolve the case, and it is prudence that dictates what can or should be done concerning the practice of this virtue.

Fraternally Correcting Others

Q. Is fraternal correction an act of charity?

A. Yes. We have counted it among spiritual acts of charity.

Q. What is the proper order to be observed in fraternal correction so that it is an act of true charity?

A. The following must be considered: Whether the fault is public or secret. If it is hidden, secrecy must be maintained and the correction made privately. Since charity is the driving force behind the correction, for it to be a true act of charity, the interest of the person and the common good must be taken into account. Love seeks and ponders all possible means that are most conducive to helping the neighbor improve. If one cannot assist the other person by oneself, one should make use of other friends, unless the fault is so secret that it doesn't allow for anyone else to be involved. If the correction would lead to a greater harm for the person, it should be postponed, the fault tolerated, and prayers offered instead. If there is hope for improvement or benefit, gentle means inspired by charity should be applied. If the fault is public, the correction should be made public; the individual should be admonished one, two, or three times, either personally or through others, with great love and kindness. If the person does not listen and the scandal can be tolerated, prayer, patience, and tolerance should be employed. There are faults that people only correct over time, as circumstances change and the opportunity for improvement arises. If the fault is scandalous, one must consider whether the scandal is tolerable or not. If it does not cause serious damage to the common good of religion or the state, it should be tolerated, because the force of authority should not be employed in correcting the sinner, except after all means of mercy, love, and kindness have been exhausted by charity. If the scandal is intolerable, after applying the means dictated by charity, it should be restrained by justice. In this case, the matter should first be reported to the prelate. The prelate should, as a father and good shepherd, provide all warnings and admonitions inspired by love. If the scandal does not require an immediate remedy, the prelate should exhaust, as a representative of the Church, which is the most tender and affectionate of all mothers, all the resources of charity. If the harm is bearable, time should be given to allow it to pass and to wait patiently for God to open a way for conversion. If the admonitions are not heeded, the tools of justice should be employed, and the offender judged according to all the formalities of the law, at least those essential to judicial jurisdiction. This order is essential for paternal and fraternal correction to be a true spiritual act of charity, and therefore an act of benevolence and charity.

Q. Is fraternal correction only the responsibility of prelates and priests?

A. It is an obligation for everyone, with the difference being that priests do it as part of their ministry and laypeople due to the strict commandment of charity.

Q. Are prelates, civil authorities, and magistrates obligated to correct public scandals?

A. Yes. It is their responsibility. And parents have the same obligation toward their children.

Q. Can and should subjects correct their prelates?

A. Yes, but with respect and reverence, taking into account the circumstances, the nature of the matter, and the status of the individuals involved.

Lesson 46: Vices Opposing Charity

Q. How many and which are the vices opposed to charity?

A. The main one is hatred, which opposes love. Envy goes against joy. Discord, strife, quarrels, turmoil, sedition, war, and schism oppose peace. And scandal opposes benevolence.

Q. How can hatred be considered?

A. It can be against God and against our neighbors. A person can fall into the sin of hatred against God, considering God as the universal legislator and ruler who punishes criminals and the guilty.

Q. Where is the fault in hatred against our neighbors?

A. In hating in them what they have from God, such as being, living, and all the gifts of nature and grace within them. Hating in people what they have of guilt, evil, and flaws is not a sin.

Q. Is hatred the greatest of all sins?

A. Yes, because it opposes the noblest, most excellent, and queen of all virtues.

Q. What is laziness or sloth?

A. It is a decline of the will to do good or a sadness that weighs down and oppresses a person and restrains them from doing good deeds.

Q. What does laziness oppose?

A. In the sense we explained, it goes against charity since joy is an effect of this virtue.

Q. Is it a capital vice?

A. Yes, because it is the root and cause of many others.

Q. What is envy?

A. It is an excessive sadness over the good fortune of others.

This vice consists of a person being grieved by the prosperity and happiness of their neighbor, being saddened by what should bring them joy.

Q. Is it a capital vice?

A. Yes. It gives rise to other vices, such as murmuring, slander, and defamation, joy in seeing one's neighbor oppressed, and sadness in knowing their prosperity.

Q. What is schism?

A. It is a vice opposed to charity, in which a person separates themselves from the moral body of the Church. This can happen by either refusing to submit to the Church's head or not wanting to communicate with its members.

Q. Is war a vice or sin?

A. It can be lawful, and it is when the common good requires it.

Q. What is scandal?

A. It is an improper saying or action that leads others to ruin or downfall.

Q. In how many ways is there scandal?

A. In two ways: Pharisaic scandal and scandal of the weak. The first comes from malice, and the second from ignorance or weakness. There is active scandal and passive scandal. The active scandal involves the one who causes the downfall, and the passive scandal involves the one who falls into the trap or precipice that the other has prepared.

Q. Should we abstain from actions that are inherently good to avoid scandal?

A. If the scandal is Pharisaic, no. However, if it arises from ignorance or weakness, the actions can be hidden or postponed until explanations have been given to help remove their ignorance. If after providing explanations they are still scandalized, the scandal can be considered Pharisaic. In these situations, prudence should consider the circumstances of individuals and the issue at hand, whether good deeds are obligatory, if the good is common and public, if they are a supererogation, etc.

Q. Is scandal a sin?

A. Yes. It goes against the love of one's neighbors and attacks benevolence.

Lesson 47: Gifts of the Holy Spirit

Having discussed what virtues are, let's talk about each of the gifts in particular.

Q. What are the gifts of the Holy Spirit?

A. They are qualities infused into the soul that prepare all the human's powers for following the guidance of the Holy Spirit.

Q. How many are they?

A. There are seven: wisdom, understanding, counsel, knowledge, fortitude, piety, and fear of God.

Q. What is the gift of understanding?

A. It is an infused quality by which the human's intellect is fortified and confirmed to view, contemplate, and meditate on the objects proposed by faith.

Q. What is the gift of wisdom?

A. It is an infused quality by which a person forms a certain and right judgment of God and divine things.

Q. What is the gift of knowledge?

A. It is an infused quality through which a person forms a correct and certain judgment on human things and created objects, distinguishing what must be believed and what must not be believed.

Q. What is the gift of counsel?

A. It is an infused quality in the soul by which reason is fortified, helped, and prepared by the Holy Spirit to inquire, seek, judge, and dictate everything appropriate to be done in order to achieve the ultimate end.

Q. Which powers do these four gifts perfect?

A. The intellectual powers.

Q. Which virtues do they belong to?

A. The gift of understanding and the gift of knowledge belong to faith; the gift of wisdom belongs to charity, and the gift of counsel to prudence.

Q. What is the gift of piety?

A. It is an infused quality in the soul by which a person is disposed and moved by the Holy Spirit to give God the love, affection, and respect due to him as the universal Father of all humans.

Q. What is the gift of fortitude?

A. It is an infused quality in the soul by which a person is moved, fortified, and prepared by the Holy Spirit to progress towards their ultimate end despite all the dangers, evils, pains, and torments that may be encountered on their journey.

Q. To which virtue does this gift belong?

A. To fortitude.

Q. What is the gift of fear of God?

A. It is an infused quality in the soul through which a person is moved by the Holy Spirit to submit to God, respect him as a superior, and fear him as a Father.

Q. In how many ways can fear be considered?

A. There is chaste and filial fear, servile fear, and evil and worldly fear. Only filial fear is a gift of the Holy Spirit.

Q. To which virtue does this gift belong?

A. To hope and also to temperance.

Excellence of Virtues and Gifts

Q. Are virtues more excellent than gifts?

A. Supernatural or theological virtues are more noble than gifts because they are given to help and perfect virtues. Gifts are more excellent than natural virtues.

Q. Among the virtues, is there any more excellent than the others?

A. Yes. Intellectual virtues are more excellent than moral ones. Among all the moral virtues, there are four that are more important than the others and they are: prudence, justice, fortitude, and temperance. Theological virtues exceed in dignity moral and intellectual virtues.

Q. Which is the most important of all virtues?

A. Charity is the queen. It gives form to all virtues. Aided by the seven gifts of the Holy Spirit, like its ministers, it moves, directs, and elevates all the forces, actions, and life of a person towards their ultimate end, which is God.

Section Three: Virtues Considered in Individuals

Lesson 48: Social Virtues

We have already defined what virtue is when considered in itself. We have contemplated all the different types into which it is divided. We have talked about them collectively and each one individually. Now it is time to look at them in their subjects. Let's now contemplate them in their degrees of perfection, and in all the states, classes, and roles within society.

Q. In how many ways can a person be considered?

A. Two: as an individual and as a member of a family or part of the social body.

Looking at human beings as members of society, they are obligated to practice certain virtues that would not be necessary if they were solitary. Let's see what these are. The perfection of the social body demands that each person occupies their own place and exercises the roles and functions that are proper to them.

In the following Lessons, to understand the virtues that people are obligated to acquire as members of the social body, we will examine these three points: 1) The different roles and functions of this body; 2) their states; 3) their various degrees of perfection. Having examined these, we will become convinced that, in the practice and exercise of virtues, people must pay attention not only to those virtues they must practice as individuals but also to all those that are appropriate for their role, their state, and their level of perfection. Coming to the first point:

Q. How many ways of life are there?

A. Three: active life, contemplative life, and a mixed life of action and contemplation.

Q. What does the active life consist of?

A. The active life is primarily found in all those members of the social body who have their functions and roles for the exercise of arts and trades. To understand this more clearly, we must keep in mind that this body has infinite needs, which must be met by created, organized, and well-functioning members. This social body needs food and drink. Agriculture, using the rules of the art, presents the fruits of labor on the table. Here we have infinite members dedicated to this purpose. The social body needs clothing; many factories and machines produce silk, cotton, linen, hemp, and wool. Tailors, shoemakers, hat makers, and countless other craftspeople organize their work for this need. To protect the social body from the inclemencies of weather, architecture is necessary, and roles are assigned to bricklayers, carpenters, iron, steel, lead, and other metal manufacturers. The social body needs guidance towards happiness: for temporal and material matters, all the political and civil governance structures have their ordered offices, ministries, and functions; and for eternal and spiritual matters, the ecclesiastical governments. For support during illness, there are medical professionals, medicine, surgery, and pharmaceutical services. To exercise these roles, education is necessary, and here we have many schools, institutes, seminaries, etc.

The active life, then, consists of carrying out the role, function, or ministry that each person exercises in the social body.

Q. What virtues should those in the active life practice?

A. Each member should exercise their functions according to the objective they are directed towards. Those leading an active life must organize their life, actions, and virtues to fulfill the duties of their state. They must practice those virtues that correspond to their position and let go of the exercise of other virtues that are incompatible with their state.

Q. Provide a practical example.

A. The farmer and gardener must sanctify their work by tilling the land. Spending long hours in church and attending religious services are acts of virtue. However, if these are not obligatory for them, and they consume their working days, it could be detrimental to their livelihood. Under this consideration, acts of virtue that are praiseworthy for some people may be blameworthy for others.

Q. Is the active life necessary for the social body?

A. Yes. The social body needs to eat, drink, dress, and meet its physical and spiritual needs, and without the active life, it would perish in misery. By organizing life, actions, and virtues to meet the physical needs of society, one serves the public and common good. If this is done for God, the active life becomes a continuous exercise of beneficence. Beneficence, as we have said, is a virtue that belongs to charity, which orders the active life for the good of our neighbors.

of creatures, while people need to be directed and guided towards their happiness. Intermediaries and subordinates are needed, and these are: political, civil, military, and economic governments for temporal happiness and ecclesiastical, monastic, and religious governments for eternal happiness.

Q: What are the specific virtues of those who govern?

A: As the common good is the object of their actions, offices, and functions, prudence, justice, and acts of charity are the virtues that should shine in them.

Q: Does the ministry of authorities belong to an active, contemplative, or mixed life?

A: They are ministers whose actions are ordered towards the governance of society, which belongs to the active life. It can also be a ministry of mixed life if the one administering also shares and gives what they have received in contemplation.

Q: What virtues should a head of a family possess?

A: Prudence, charity, and other virtues of good governance.

Q: Are the virtues of those who govern the same as those of their subjects?

A: No. There is a significant difference between being the driving force and being part of the machinery. Obedience, humility, and submission are necessary virtues for subjects. Fidelity to higher orders, exactness, and promptness in carrying out the commands of those who govern are virtues that distinguish them from the governed.

Lesson 51: States of the Social Body

Q. What is a state?

A. A state is a way of life or a manner of living that brings stability, firmness, constancy, and immobility.

Q. What is the difference between a state and an office?

A. An office is not stable, while a state is, as indicated by its name.

Q. Are there different states in the social body?

A. Yes, there are.

Q. What are they?

A. The state of marriage, the ecclesiastical state, and the religious state.

Q. Why and how are these states?

A. A person is bound to marriage by the laws of contract and the Church; the ecclesiastical state is also binding through holy orders, and the religious state is binding through solemn vows.

Q. What about those who are not bound by the laws of marriage, holy orders, or solemn vows? What are they called?

A. They are called single or free.

Q. Who should be consulted to discern one's vocation?

A. First and foremost, God. He is the author of the social body, having created each member and organized it. He alone knows the proper place for each person in the body and the role they should play. It is up to God alone to inspire and direct the state and office that one should choose.

Q. Is a person free to choose or not choose a state or to choose one state over another?

A. In this matter, a person is perfectly free and not subject to anyone, neither are children subject to their parents, nor servants to their masters, nor subjects to their superiors. Any harassment, humiliation, or oppression in this regard is barbaric and cruel. Parents and superiors cannot, under any pretext, interfere in the slightest with this freedom.

Q. Can a person make the right choice in choosing their state?

A. If one wants to act rationally and sensibly, God - the author of the natural and supernatural order of the social body - will provide enough signs for them to recognize their calling, and if they do not succeed, it will always be their own fault. There are natural inclinations, tendencies, and many special internal calls to which a person can pay attention. Just as a vine is created to produce grapes and follows a natural order to achieve this purpose; just as each plant, from the day it is planted or sown, naturally tends toward producing leaves, branches, and fruit according to its species; just as in the natural body each member shows signs from the moment of creation for the function for which it is organized and ordered, so too can people, if they pay attention to their natural and supernatural inclinations and tendencies, learn the state and office they should

156

hold in the social body, as they have been created, organized, prepared, and ordered by the Author of that very body. When God calls a member of the body for a particular function, He provides all the necessary dispositions, all natural and supernatural graces and gifts required by that state or office.

Furthermore, God makes known His will and reveals it through His works and deeds. One who is born poor and common should not presume they are called to be a king, and if God wanted them to be so, He would reveal His will through His works and deeds.

Q. Are the virtues of singles the same as those of married people, clergy, and religious?

A. Considered generally, everyone should possess all virtues; but each state and office has its own specific virtues, without which they would be failing in their duties.

Q. What virtues are specific to singles, married people, clergy, and religious?

A. The brief scope of our work does not allow us to elaborate further on this Lesson. Please consult ascetic doctors who have written extensively on this subject.

Lesson 52: Virtues in Various Degrees of Perfection

We have already seen that in the social body there are different offices, functions, and states; we agree that in the practice of virtues, a person should consider their state and office and should adapt to their position in exercising them, seeking and acquiring those that are proper for their perfection. We would like to know how virtues are found in several individuals of the same state and office; or, to put it better, I would like to know if the same virtues are found in the social body in various and different degrees of perfection.

A. There is no doubt. Virtue is present in the social body in different degrees of perfection. We see this in the animal body. Powers and senses are very weak, feeble, and imperfect in the first moment of their organization. At birth, the body is already stronger, and until the age of thirty, it grows continuously in strength, vigor, and natural virtue. The vigor, strength, and natural virtue are found and seen in different degrees of perfection in different bodies. Charity and all the virtues that accompany it are seen in different degrees of perfection in the states and offices of the social body.

Q. Should one practice virtues according to the degree of perfection they have?

A. Yes. And knowing this is so important that ignorance and confusion can cause serious harm to the spirit. If a child wanted to lift a weight that a strong man moves, they would be discouraged and fall into despair. If a beginner in virtue practices or presumes to practice the works of a perfect man, being beyond their strength, they will fall into the same despair. A child must act in one way, and a young man in another. "When I was a child," said the Apostle St. Paul, "I spoke like a child; when I became a man, I put away childish things" (1 Cor 13:11).

Q. What are these degrees of perfection?

A. We have already briefly discussed this in Lesson 7.

Q. So, in the practice and exercise of virtues, should a person pay attention to and consider their state, their office, and their strength?

A. They certainly should, and if they don't, they expose themselves to commit many excesses. Virtues do not destroy the social body, but rather - be it political and civil, moral and religious - they perfect it in all its functions, offices, ministries, acts, and actions. Virtue perfects a person gradually, over time, through exercise, according to their state, office, and vocation.

Q. Do miracles, prophecies, gift of tongues, and other similar graces serve as a sure sign of perfection and holiness?

A. Not at all. Being gratuitous gifts, God can give them to the perfect and imperfect, the weak and the strong; and they cannot be taken as a certain and infallible sign of sanctity and perfection of a person, because it is virtues that perfect a person, and all these graces are not virtues, but means to acquire virtue, to authorize it, support it, and preserve it. See about this what St. John of the Cross has written.

Complementary Text

1st Proposition: Method is one of the inherent laws of any teaching plan. - Development of our philosophical-religious teaching plan. Refutation of eclecticism. - Foundations of this teaching.

2nd Proposition: There are criteria that demonstrate the existence of certainty. - Refutation of Skepticism.

3rd Proposition: Once the existence of this certainty is demonstrated, it is a property of man to inquire where it exists. - Refutation of Indifferentism.

4th Proposition: The inquiry of this certainty will give us, as a first result, the existence and unity of the first principle. - Refutation of Atheism and Manichaeism.

5th Proposition: The analysis of Nature has given us the certainty that, in addition to the order of cosmological phenomena, there is the order of psychological phenomena. - Refutation of Materialism.

6th Proposition: This analysis has also shown us that there are existences belonging to the psychological order and independent of the cosmological order. Such is the first principle. - Refutation of Pantheism.

7th Proposition: This analysis has shown us that there are existences belonging to the cosmological order and independent of the psychological order. - Refutation of Spiritualism.

8th Proposition: This same analysis has shown us that

there are existences belonging to both the psychological and cosmological orders, such as human beings. - Refutation of Organicism and Philosophical Unitarianism.

9th Proposition: Since all things have come from the first principle, the first Principle must be Omnipotent. - Refutation of Theism.

10th Proposition: Providence is another of the properties inherent in the idea of the first principle. - Refutation of Deism.

11th Proposition: Justice is another of the properties inherent in the idea of the first Principle. - Refutation of Protestantism in relation to this theory.

12th Proposition: Sound philosophy of all ages has agreed that the first principle was the Truth. - Refutation of Skepticism in relation to this principle.

13th Proposition: Every being belonging to the psychological order has as an inherent property of its own activity the principle of responsibility and, consequently, the principle of freedom. - Refutation of Fatalism and Determinism. - Examination of Phrenology.

14th Proposition: Immortality is another inherent principle of every being endowed with its own activity, according to this principle: God and the soul are immortal. - Refutation of Materialism.

15th Proposition: There are relationships between humans and the First Principle. -Refutation of Theism.

16th Proposition: These relationships are founded on the principles of Reason on the part of humans, and on those of Revelation on the part of God. -Refutation of Naturalism.

17th Proposition: Revelation is a fact. -Refutation of Deism.

18th Proposition: This Revelation was communicated to us in ancient times through the Mosaic Law and in modern times through the Evangelical Law. -1st part: Refutation of Naturalism. -2nd part: Refutation of Judaism.

19th Proposition: The miracles performed in favor of the Mosaic doctrine are proof of its divinity; those performed in favor of the Evangelical doctrine are also proof of its divinity. -Refutation of Naturalism.

20th Proposition: The fulfillment of prophecies in the Mosaic doctrine is another proof of its divinity; the holiness of the Evangelical doctrine is also another proof of its divinity. -Refutation of anti-religion.

21st Proposition: There is complete harmony between Reason and Revelation. -Refutation of Philosophism.

22nd Proposition: The theories inscribed in the books of the Mosaic Law and the true principles of modern sciences are in complete harmony. -Refutation of some false assertions of modern philosophy.

23rd Proposition: A Church is necessary as the depository of the Evangelical doctrine. -Refutation of free examination.

24th Proposition: The Church, as the depository of the Evangelical doctrine, must be justified by the testimonies of Revelation and supported by the criteria of Reason.

-Refutation of Socinianism.

25th Proposition: Only the Church, justified by these testimonies and supported by these criteria, can reveal to us the relationships of humans with the First Principle, and must therefore uphold the Principle of religious intolerance. -Refutation of Tolerantism.

26th Proposition: This Church must be a morally perfect body. Refutation of Protestantism.

27th Proposition: The principle of authority is a necessity in this Church. -Refutation of liberal Protestantism and against Anglicanism.

28th Proposition: Given these last two theories, legislative power and, as a consequence, coercive power must be admitted in the Church. -Refutation of some modern assertions.

29th Proposition: As a consequence of the legislative power, judicial jurisdiction must also reside in the Church and, therefore, the power to require ecclesiastical courts. -Against some modern theories.

30th Proposition: The Inquisition, according to these principles, is the exercise of one of the rights of the Church. -Against Puigblanc in his Inquisición sin máscara (Inquisition without a mask).

31st Proposition: The Pope, speaking ex cathedra, is an infallible judge in matters of faith and morals.

32nd Proposition: Catholicism, with the dogma of original sin, explains the true cause of the current degeneration. -Against Phalansterianism.

33rd Proposition: The penitentiary system, adopted by the Catholic Church and authorized by Jesus Christ, is highly rational and in accordance with the principles of humanity. -Against Protestantism.

Application of these philosophical-Catholic theories: General Thesis

34th Proposition: The established principles with all their consequences influence the material, intellectual, and moral progress of humanity. -Vindication of the label of backwardness applied to the Church.

35th Proposition: Catholic theories explicitly prescribe the preservation and even material perfection of the individual. -Refutation of suicide and dueling.

36th Proposition: Catholic theories contribute and even prescribe the most perfect organization and the highest preservation of societies. -Refutation of Socialism and Communism.

37th Proposition: The right to association is guaranteed in nature itself. -Jean-Jacques Rousseau in his Social Contract.

38th Proposition: The right to family is guaranteed in the right to association. -Against revolutionary principles.

39th Proposition: Religious communities are also guaranteed by the right to association. -Against anti-monastic ideas.

40th Proposition: Christian principles, which are the principles of perfectibility taken to the highest degree; the attractiveness of their worship; the entire Catholic history, show how much artistic advancements and all material

164

progress owe to this Religion, the greatest promoter of human activity. -Vindication of the label of obscurantism applied to the Church.

41st Proposition: Catholic theories, by connecting the psychological order with the cosmological order and linking the phenomena known by reason with the unknown but certain phenomena of Revelation, is the principle of sound philosophy. -Refutation of Kantism and Rationalism.

42nd Proposition: History also shows us that Catholic principles promote intellectual progress. -Refutation of some assertions by Charles Villiers.

43rd Proposition: The principle of authority, as established by the Church, also promotes intellectual progress. -Against the disciples of free examination.

44th Proposition: The freedom fostered by Catholic principles is another guarantee offered by Catholicism to intellectual progress. -Against the assertions of the disciples of free examination.

45th Proposition: Catholic doctrine is eminently civilizing. -Refutation of some modern theories.

46th Proposition: The principle of authority has guided modern civilization. -Refutation of some assertions by Mr. Guizot.

47th Proposition: The doctrines of Catholic intolerance have served as a counterbalance to barbarism. -Refutation of some theories by the aforementioned Mr. Guizot.

48th Proposition: The Inquisition, which according to Balmes is nothing more than the application of the doctrine of intolerance to a particular case, has also prevented heresy and impiety from obstructing the civilizing march of the Catholic Church. -Refutation of Mr. Jercal in his 'Mysteries of the Inquisition.'

49th Proposition: The priest is the preceptor of civilization. -Against the detractors of the priesthood.

50th Proposition: Convents, as centers of education and morality, have consequently been centers of civilization. -Against detractors of monks.

51st Proposition: Jesuit colleges, renowned for their education which is the foundation of morality, have been and continue to be centers of civilization. -Against anti-Jesuitism.

52nd Proposition: The practices of religious brotherhoods, far from fostering fanaticism, promote morality. -Against detractors of religious associations.

Thank you!

We greatly value your feedback on this book and invite you to share your thoughts with us. As a growing independent publishing company, we are constantly striving to enhance the quality of our publications.

To make it easy for you to provide your insights, the QR code located to the right will directly lead you to the Amazon review page, where you can share your experience and offer any suggestions for improvement that you may have.

Related books

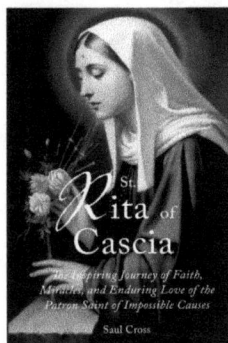

Dominic Savio
The Child Saint of Heroic Virtue
Saul Cross

Padre Pio
Encounters and Miraculous Healings
A Journey Through the Life of a Modern Saint
Saul Cross

St. Rita of Cascia
The Inspiring Journey of Faith, Miracles, and Enduring Love of the Patron Saint of Impossible Causes
Saul Cross

Scan the QR code below to browse our selection of related books and access exclusive supplemental materials:

9 798399 716572